SCAMPROOF

The Guide to Spotting and Avoiding Modern Scams

James T. Blake

About the Book

'ScamProof' was written with one mission in mind: to empower you with knowledge that could protect your money, your identity, and your peace of mind.

In a world where scams are becoming more sophisticated by the day, from fake investment schemes and online shopping traps to emotional manipulation and digital fraud, this book serves as your simple, no-nonsense survival guide. Whether you're tech-savvy or not, rich or broke, young or old, you're a potential target. And this book will show you how to avoid becoming a victim.

What makes this book different?

- Clear and Easy to Understand: No confusing jargon or overly technical talk, just real-world explanations, examples, and red flags to watch for.

- Extensive Yet Practical: Covers a wide variety of scams across financial, emotional, digital, and consumer domains, with actionable steps for prevention.

- For Everyone: Whether you're a student, a retiree, a business owner, or just someone trying to navigate the online world, the content is designed with you in mind.

- Updated Thinking: Includes modern scams involving crypto, AI, social media, and digital payment platforms: things many older guides overlook.

In short, this book doesn’t just tell you what scams exist. It teaches you how they work and why they succeed, so you can stay one step ahead.

Knowledge is your best defense. Let this book be your shield.

Table of Contents:

Investment & Financial Scams

Table of Contents:

Consumer & Online Shopping Scams

Table of Contents:

Relationship & Emotional Manipulation Scams

Table of Contents:

Housing & Real Estate Scams

Table of Contents:

Employment & Business Scams

Table of Contents:

Education & Scholarship Scams

Table of Contents:

Government-Related & Legal Scams

Table of Contents:

Tech & Digital Scams

Table of Contents:

Disaster & Charity Scams

Table of Contents:

Final Words

Investment & Financial scams

- **Ponzi Schemes**

Paying returns to earlier investors with newer investors' money.

- **Pyramid Schemes**

Earning primarily through recruitment rather than selling a product.

- **Pump-and-Dump Scams**

Inflating stock/crypto prices before selling off.

- **Forex and Binary Options Scams**

Promising huge returns through currency/option trading.

- **Fake Crypto Projects / Rug Pulls**

Crypto tokens launched with no intention of long-term development.

- **Advance Fee Fraud**

Promising wealth in exchange for upfront payment.

- **“High Yield Investment Programs” (HYIPs)**

Unregistered investments claiming to deliver sky-high returns.

- **Boiler Room Scams**

Aggressive sales tactics used to sell worthless investments.

- **Fake Gold / Precious Metal Investments**

Scams involving counterfeit or overpriced metals.

- **Cash Gifting Schemes**

Illegal gifting circles that collapse quickly.

Ponzi Schemes:
The Illusion of Easy Money

What Is a Ponzi Scheme?

A Ponzi scheme is a type of investment scam where returns to earlier investors are paid using money contributed by newer investors, rather than from actual profits generated by legitimate business activities.

There's usually no real investment happening - just a constant cycle of recruiting new victims to keep the illusion alive.

Named after Charles Ponzi, who scammed thousands in the 1920s by promising 50% returns in 90 days through international postal coupons, this scheme has evolved and resurfaced in countless forms since then.

How It Works

1. A Promoter Promises High Returns

® The scammer claims to have a secret, fail-proof investment strategy.
® They promise unusually high and consistent profits.

2. Early Investors Are Paid with New Money

® These early investors actually receive payouts, which makes the scheme seem real.
® Word of mouth helps attract more people.

3. The Scheme Grows. And Becomes Fragile

® It relies on a constant influx of new investors.
® Once new recruitment slows, the scheme collapses.

4. The Collapse

® When too many people try to cash out, or new money stops coming in, the scheme falls apart.
® Most victims lose everything.

Common Red Flags

- “Guaranteed returns” with no risk
- Consistently high returns, even when markets are down
- Difficulty withdrawing funds
- Lack of transparency about how profits are generated
- Unregistered investments or secretive strategies
- Pressure to “reinvest” instead of cashing out

Common Red Flags

- “Guaranteed returns” with no risk
- Consistently high returns, even when markets are down
- Difficulty withdrawing funds
- Lack of transparency about how profits are generated
- Unregistered investments or secretive strategies
- Pressure to “reinvest” instead of cashing out

Real-World Example: Bernie Madoff

Perhaps the most infamous modern Ponzi scheme was run by Bernie Madoff, who defrauded investors of over $65 billion. His fund paid old investors using the money of new ones for decades, until it all came crashing down in 2008.

Many of his victims were charities, retirement funds, and ordinary people who trusted his reputation.

How to Protect Yourself

Verify investment firms and advisors with regulatory bodies (like the SEC or FINRA in the U.S.)

Be skeptical of investments that promise consistent, above-average returns

Ask questions: If you don't understand how it works, don't invest

Avoid secrecy: Real investments should have clear, transparent documentation

Don't be rushed: Scammers often create urgency to stop you from thinking it through

Pyramid Schemes: The Trap of Endless Recruitment

What Is a Pyramid Scheme?

A pyramid scheme is a scam disguised as a business opportunity where earnings come not from selling real products or services, but from recruiting new participants. Each new recruit pays money to the person who recruited them, with the promise that they can make money the same way: by bringing in more people.

It looks like a triangle or pyramid:
The people at the top make money as long as new people keep joining at the bottom.

Eventually, the scheme collapses, because you run out of people to recruit.

How It Works

1. You Pay to Join

® You're asked to "invest," buy a starter kit, or pay a joining fee.
® You're told you'll make money by signing others up to do the same.

2. You Recruit Others

® Your "income" depends on how many people you recruit, not what you sell.
® New recruits are then told to recruit more people.

3. It Grows Fast. Then Crashes

® The structure grows exponentially (each person recruiting 2, then 4, then 8...).
® Eventually, there are no more people left to join.
® The last people to join lose everything.

Red Flags to Watch For

- Heavy focus on recruitment over product sales
- Promises of income from bringing in others, not from selling a product
- High-pressure tactics to "join now or miss out"
- Claims of unlimited earning potential without real evidence
- Vague or overpriced products that are rarely bought by outsiders
- Being paid more to recruit than to sell

Pyramid Scheme vs. MLM (Multi-Level Marketing)

Not all MLMs are illegal, but many walk a very thin line.

Feature	Pyramid Scheme	Legal MLM
Main focus	Recruitment	Selling products
Income source	New recruits' fees	Product sales
Product demand	Often none	Should be real and in demand
Sustainability	Eventually collapses	Can be long-term if legit

If you're not sure whether something is a pyramid scheme, ask:
"Would I make money if I didn't recruit anyone?"
If the answer is no, it's likely a pyramid scheme.

Real-World Examples

BurnLounge (2000s): Sold music through a "network," but most income came from recruiting others. Shut down by the FTC.

Women Empowering Women (1990s): Claimed to be a “gifting circle,” but was a pyramid scheme targeting women with promises of sisterhood and riches.

Modern Social Media “Circles”: Variations of pyramid schemes disguised as group gifts, often shared on Facebook, Instagram, or TikTok.

How to Protect Yourself

Ask how people make money: If it's mostly from recruitment, walk away.

Check product demand: Are real customers buying it, or just recruits?

Research the company: Look up lawsuits, reviews, or government warnings.

Trust your gut: If something feels shady or too good to be true, it probably is.

Watch out for “Gifting Circles” or “Blessing Looms”. These are just pyramid schemes in disguise.

Pump-and-Dump Scams: The Hype Before the Crash

What Is a Pump-and-Dump Scam?

A pump-and-dump scam is a type of market manipulation where scammers artificially inflate the price of a stock or cryptocurrency ("pump") through false or misleading claims. Once the price rises and unsuspecting investors buy in, the scammers sell off their holdings ("dump") at the inflated price - causing the value to crash.

Victims are left holding worthless assets.

How It Works

1. Scammers Buy Cheap

® The fraudsters quietly purchase large amounts of a low-value asset (often a penny stock or new crypto token).

2. They Create Hype

® Through social media, email blasts, or online forums, they spread misleading info:

- “Big news is coming!”
- “This is the next Bitcoin!”
- “Get in before it explodes!”

® Sometimes influencers or bots are used to amplify the hype.

3. Price Goes Up (The Pump)

® As more people buy in due to FOMO (fear of missing out), the price surges.

4. Scammers Sell (The Dump)

® Once the price is high, scammers sell all their holdings.

® The market is flooded with sell orders, causing the price to crash.

5. Everyone Else Loses

® Late investors are left with worthless assets and no way to recover their money.

Red Flags to Watch For

- Sudden spikes in price without news or company updates
- “Get rich quick” buzz on Reddit, Telegram, Discord, or Twitter/X
- Unsolicited investment advice from strangers or influencers
- Lack of real business or project behind the asset
- Thinly traded assets with low volume and liquidity
- Use of phrases like “moon,” “Lambo soon,” or “10x overnight”

Common Platforms for Pump-and-Dump

- Cryptocurrency tokens: Especially new or obscure ones on platforms like Binance Smart Chain or Ethereum.

- Penny stocks: Low-priced, low-volume stocks listed outside of major exchanges.

- NFTs: Fake hype used to inflate price before the creator disappears.

Real-World Examples

Wolf of Wall Street (1990s): Jordan Belfort's firm, Stratton Oakmont, pumped worthless stocks to defraud investors. Made famous by the movie.

Bitconnect (2016–2018): Promised high crypto returns through a fake trading bot. Its token value crashed from over $400 to nearly zero in weeks.

Squid Game Token (2021): Based on the popular Netflix show, this token soared and then crashed in a matter of days. The developers vanished with millions.

How to Protect Yourself

Do your own research (DYOR): Don't trust hype alone. Look into the fundamentals.

Avoid FOMO: Be cautious when a project suddenly gains attention out of nowhere.

Check liquidity and volume: If few people are trading the asset, it's risky.

Be skeptical of anonymous teams: If the creators won't show their faces, that's a red flag.

üUse trusted exchanges: Stick with regulated platforms and don't invest in unknown assets.

Forex & Binary Options Scams: False Promises in Fast-Paced Markets

What Are Forex and Binary Options?

® Forex (Foreign Exchange) trading involves buying and selling currencies to profit from changing exchange rates.

® Binary Options are a type of financial "bet" where you predict whether an asset's price will go up or down within a short time frame (often 30 seconds to a few minutes).

Both markets are legitimate, but they're also breeding grounds for scams, especially when marketed to beginners.

What Makes These Scams So Dangerous?

Scammers exploit the complexity and fast-moving nature of these markets to fool people with promises like:

® "Double your money in a week!"
® "100% guaranteed profits using our system!"
® "No experience needed, our robot trades for you!"

In reality, most victims lose their deposits and are unable to withdraw funds.

How It Works

1. The Lure

® Victims are targeted through ads, social media DMs, or fake testimonials.
® Scammers show screenshots of huge profits or "luxury" lifestyles.

2. The Sign-Up

® You're told to deposit money into an online trading platform (usually unregulated).
® You may be given access to a fake trading dashboard that shows you're "winning."

3. Manipulated Outcomes

® Binary options platforms often control the outcome: Even if you make correct predictions, you lose.
® With forex, scammers may fake trades or deliberately wipe your account using high-risk trades.

4. The Withdrawal Trap

® When you try to cash out, you're asked to:

- Pay a "release" fee
- Deposit more to "verify your account"
- r you're simply ignored and blocked

Red Flags to Watch For

- "Guaranteed returns" or fixed daily profits
- Unregulated platforms (not registered with financial authorities)
- High-pressure sales tactics or limited-time "offers"
- Claims of AI or bots that "never lose"
- Requests for payment via crypto, gift cards, or wire transfers
- No real information about the company or its owners

Real-World Examples

OptionRally & Banc de Binary: These now-defunct platforms scammed thousands with rigged trading interfaces and refused withdrawals.

Mirror Trading International (MTI): A fake forex bot promising 10% monthly returns. Collapsed in 2020, costing investors over $1 billion.

Instagram Trading Gurus: Many self-proclaimed "mentors" show rented cars and fake screenshots to lure followers into shady forex platforms.

How to Protect Yourself

Check registration: Verify the broker is licensed with a recognized financial authority (e.g. FCA, CFTC, ASIC).

Avoid unregulated platforms: If the broker isn't clearly regulated, stay away.

Start small, test withdrawals: Try withdrawing a small amount early. If they stall or refuse, that's a red flag.

Never believe 100% win-rate bots or systems

Research the platform: Look for reviews, warnings from regulators, and scam reports online.

Fake Crypto Projects & Rug Pulls: When the Developers Disappear

What Is a Rug Pull?

In the world of cryptocurrency, a rug pull is when developers create a new crypto token or decentralized finance (DeFi) project, hype it up, collect investor money, and then vanish with the funds, leaving investors with worthless tokens.

Think of it like pulling the rug out from under your feet: suddenly and without warning.

How It Works

1. Create a Token

® Scammers launch a flashy new coin (e.g., "MoonDogeAI" or "ShibaRocketX").

® It's listed on decentralized exchanges (like Uniswap or PancakeSwap) where anyone can add tokens.

2. Hype the Project

® Promises of insane returns, vague roadmaps, and flashy websites.

® Paid influencers or bots flood social media with buzz.

® Fake partnerships, celebrity endorsements, or "audit" reports are often faked.

3. Liquidity Trap

® Investors buy in and the token price skyrockets.

® Scammers lock in just enough liquidity to make trading seem legit.

4. The Rug Pull

® Developers withdraw all liquidity or mint an unlimited supply of tokens, causing the price to crash.

They vanish with millions, leaving holders with worthless tokens.

Red Flags to Watch For

- Anonymous team with no verifiable history
- No clear use case or utility for the token
- Promises of “1000x gains” or “next Dogecoin”
- Sudden token launch followed by aggressive marketing
- Code allows the creator to mint unlimited tokens or disable selling
- No audit, or audit is from an unknown or untrusted source

Real-World Examples

Squid Game Token (2021): Capitalized on the popular Netflix show. Price soared from $0.01 to over $2,800. Then collapsed to zero within minutes when developers rug-pulled.

SaveTheKids Token: Promoted by influencers, including YouTubers and streamers. Developers manipulated launch rules and dumped tokens early.

AnubisDAO (2021): Raised $60 million in liquidity for a DeFi project and disappeared within 20 hours of launch.

How to Protect Yourself

Research the team: If they're anonymous or unverifiable, be cautious.

Check the token's smart contract: Look for functions that allow minting or blacklisting users.

Verify liquidity locks: Use tools to check if the liquidity is locked and for how long.

Avoid hype coins: If it's trending just because of memes or celebrity tweets, proceed carefully.

Use reputable sources: Stick to coins listed on major exchanges with verified audits.

Advance Fee Fraud: Pay First, Lose Forever

What Is Advance Fee Fraud?

Advance fee fraud is a scam where you'r promised a large reward: money, inheritance investment returns, or even a job - but only if yo pay a fee up front. Once you pay, the scamme either disappears or keeps inventing new reason for more payments.

You never receive the promised reward.

How It Works

1. The Bait

® You receive an email, message, or letter claiming you're owed:

- A massive inheritance
- A loan approval
- A lottery win
- A business opportunity

2. The Hook

® You're asked to pay a small fee to release the funds:

- "Processing fee"
- "Legal clearance"
- "Bank transfer charge"
- "Customs tax"

3. The Repeat

® After the first payment, more fees follow:

- "Oops, another delay. Just one more fee!"
- "We need a security deposit to verify your identity."

4. The Vanish

® The scammer disappears after milking as much as possible.

® Victims are often left embarrassed and broke.

Common Variants

- Nigerian Prince Emails: Classic version where a "royal" asks for help moving money and offers a cut.
- Fake Job Offers: You're "hired" but must pay for background checks, uniforms, or training.
- Loan Scams: A "guaranteed" loan that requires upfront insurance or fees.
- Romance Scams: The online partner says they need help with visa fees, hospital bills, or travel costs.
- Lottery & Prize Scams: You "won" a prize, but must pay shipping or tax first.

Red Flags to Watch For

- Unsolicited messages promising large sums of money
- Too-good-to-be-true investment or job offers
- Requests for wire transfers, crypto, gift cards, or prepaid debit cards
- Poor grammar, odd phrasing, or overly formal language
- Pressure to act quickly or keep the deal secret

Real-World Examples

The 419 Scam (named after Nigeria’s criminal code): One of the oldest forms of advance fee fraud, still active in email inboxes today.

Fake Embassy or Visa Scams: Victims pay “processing fees” to fake immigration offices and never receive travel documents.

Romance Fraud Victims: In 2022 alone, U.S. victims of romance scams lost over $1 billion, often through advance fee fraud tactics.

How to Protect Yourself

Never pay to receive money. Legitimate institutions deduct fees from actual payouts, not before.

Verify identities. Search names, phone numbers, and company claims online.

Don't send money to strangers, even if they sound official, romantic, or desperate.

Be skeptical of urgent or emotional stories

Report fraud to your country's consumer protection or cybercrime unit.

High Yield Investment Programs (HYIPs): The Promise of Impossible Profits

What Are HYIPs?

High Yield Investment Programs (HYIPs) are fraudulent schemes that claim to offer extremely high returns (often 1–10% daily) by investing in forex, crypto, stocks, or secret "proprietary strategies." In reality, they are usually Ponzi schemes dressed up as legitimate online investment platforms.

They may run smoothly for a short time - until the scammer disappears with everyone's money.

How It Works

1. The Setup

® A slick website with dashboards, referral links, and daily "earnings."
® Claims to be an investment firm, trading platform, or AI-powered bot.

2. The Bait

® Promises of outrageous returns:
§ "Earn 5% daily with our VIP plan!"
§ "Double your money in a week!"

3. The Hook

® You're encouraged to "reinvest" your earnings instead of withdrawing.
® Referral bonuses tempt users to bring in friends and family.

4. The Collapse

® Once new deposits slow down, withdrawals are frozen.
® The site vanishes, and the scammer disappears with all the funds.

What They Claim to Invest In

- Cryptocurrency arbitrage
- Forex and commodities
- Real estate or startup funding
- Private hedge fund strategies
- “AI trading bots” or “quantum trading”

None of these are real. Most HYIPs don’t actually invest in anything, they just shuffle money between users.

Red Flags to Watch For

- Guaranteed high returns with no risk
- Anonymous team or fake corporate identity
- Recently registered website, often with poor grammar
- Referral commissions as a core feature
- Withdrawals limited to crypto or blocked after initial success
- Complex jargon with little real explanation

Real-World Examples

BitConnect (2016–2018): Claimed to offer 1% daily through a trading bot. Collapsed after hitting $2.6 billion in market cap.

Arbistar (2020): Claimed to use crypto arbitrage; froze withdrawals and disappeared with millions.

MiningMax: A fake crypto mining HYIP that stole over $250 million globally before being shut down.

How to Protect Yourself

Be realistic: No legitimate investment gives 5–10% per day.

Check regulation: HYIPs are usually unregistered and illegal in most countries.

Avoid reinvesting blindly: If you can't easily withdraw profits, that's a warning.

Look for transparency: Who runs it? Where are the investments? If you don’t know, don’t invest.

Use scam trackers: Look up reviews and blacklists before investing.

Boiler Room Scams: High-Pressure Sales for Worthless Investments

What Are Boiler Room Scams?

A boiler room scam involves a team of aggressive, often fraudulent salespeople who cold-call victims and pressure them into buying overpriced, worthless, or fake investments: usually stocks, bonds, or crypto. The name comes from the cramped, high-stress offices (like "boiler rooms") where these scammers operate.

Their goal? To talk you out of your money using charm, intimidation, and lies.

How It Works

1. The Cold Call

® Victims get a phone call or email out of the blue.

® The scammer poses as a broker, analyst, or "wealth advisor" offering an exclusive deal.

2. The Pitch

® You're told about:

- A startup "about to go public"
- A rare opportunity to get in early
- A secret tip only "select clients" are getting

® They may offer fake websites, "prospectuses," or testimonials to back it up.

3. The Pressure

® Tactics include:

- "This offer is closing today."
- "This opportunity won't come again."
- "You're smarter than most people. We only let in VIPs like you."

4. The Trap

® You wire money or send crypto to "invest."

® The scammers either:

- Disappear completely, or
- String you along with fake updates while bleeding you dry.

Real-World Boiler Room Tactics

- Fake trading platforms with dashboards that simulate real growth.
- "Recovery scams": After scamming you once, they pose as recovery agents asking for more money to get your funds back.
- International setups: Many operations are based overseas to avoid legal repercussions.

Red Flags to Watch For

- Unsolicited investment offers from unknown callers or emails
- Claims of guaranteed or insider returns
- Pressure to act immediately or keep the offer secret
- Use of fake credentials or unverifiable licenses
- Requests for payment via wire transfer, crypto, or offshore accounts

Real-World Examples

Operation Boiling Point (UK): Shut down a series of international boiler rooms selling fake carbon credits and rare earth metals to retirees.

Stratton Oakmont: The infamous real-life boiler room portrayed in *The Wolf of Wall Street*.

Asia-based boiler rooms: Ongoing global operations that target Western investors through fake stock and crypto schemes.

How to Protect Yourself

Hang up on cold calls about investments.

Verify licenses with regulatory bodies (e.g., SEC, FCA, ASIC).

Don't be flattered into investing. That's a tactic.

Search the company name + "scam" or "fraud" online.

Talk to a real financial advisor before committing funds.

Fake Gold & Precious Metal Investments: Glitter That's Actually Garbage

What Is This Scam?

Precious metals like gold, silver, platinum, and rare earth elements are often seen as "safe haven" investments. Scammers take advantage of this by selling:

- Counterfeit metals
- Overpriced products
- Nonexistent holdings
- Or fake investment schemes tied to metals

In the end, the victim either gets nothing, worthless items, or metals that are worth far less than what they paid.

How It Works

1. The Sales Pitch

® Victims are told metals are safer than stocks or crypto.

® Claims of upcoming economic collapse or hyperinflation are used to pressure investment.

2. The Offer

® The scammer offers:

- Discounted or "unreleased" gold/silver coins
- Rare metals with "guaranteed future value"
- Storage-based investments where the metals are "kept safely for you"

3. The Deception

® You may receive:

- Fake or low-quality metals
- Documents showing metal ownership, but no actual product
- Nothing at all (the scammer disappears)

Variants of the Scam

- "Allocated storage" fraud: You're told the metal is stored in your name - but no such vault exists.
- Gold IRA scams: Fake companies offer to "roll over" your retirement into precious metals. Then steal it.
- Numismatic coin fraud: Real coins, but massively overpriced due to inflated "collector" premiums.
- Mining investment scams: Fake gold mines that offer stock in a non-existent or bankrupt operation.

Red Flags to Watch Out For

- Pressure to buy during "emergencies" (economic collapse, wars, inflation)
- Unsolicited offers from phone calls or emails
- Confusing paperwork or lack of clear pricing
- Claims that the investment is 100% safe or "backed by government"
- Requests for payment via wire transfer, crypto, or untraceable methods

Real-World Examples

Merit Gold (US): Accused of overcharging seniors for collectible coins that were worth a fraction of the price.

London Gold Fix Fraud: Major banks were fined for manipulating gold prices - showing even legitimate gold markets can be risky.

"Tanzanite" scams: Promoted as rarer than diamonds, but mass-produced and sold at inflated prices.

How to Protect Yourself

Buy from reputable dealers with verifiable reviews and licenses.

Demand authentication for physical metals (certificates, assays, serial numbers).

Avoid unsolicited investment advice. Real dealers don't cold-call.

Be wary of "storage" investments. Visit or verify the vault if possible.

Know the real market price. Check daily spot prices before buying.

Cash Gifting Schemes: “Give to Receive”... But You’ll Only Give

What Are Cash Gifting Schemes?

Cash gifting schemes are scams disguised as community-based financial blessings or “wealth-building” systems. You're told to give money (often to someone above you in a “circle” or “board”), and in return, you'll eventually receive much more from future participants.

But in truth, it’s just a pyramid scheme with a warm-and-fuzzy name.

How It Works

1. The Invite

® A friend, family member, or stranger invites you to join a "gifting circle," "abundance program," or "financial blessing."

® You're told it's not a scam: it's "spiritual," "legal," or "based on ancient traditions."

2. The Initial Gift

® You're asked to "gift" a fixed amount (commonly $100, $500, or even $1,400).

® This money goes to someone already in the scheme - usually at the top of the circle.

3. The Promise

® As new people join and gift money, you'll eventually move "up the circle" and get paid by others.

® You're encouraged to recruit more people to keep the money flowing.

4. The Collapse

® Once recruitment slows down, the whole thing falls apart.

® Most participants never receive anything, except a smaller bank balance.

Common Variants

- "Women's Empowerment Circles": Marketed as sisterhood support or spiritual growth.
- "Blessing Looms" or "Money Boards": Graphic diagrams show a web of names with you at the center - only temporarily.
- "Financial Freedom Gifting Programs": Often promoted in self-help, crypto, or new-age communities.

Red Flags to Watch For

- "This is not a scam. It's gifting!" (Red flag)
- You must pay to participate or "level up"
- Emphasis on bringing in others to "unlock" your own payout
- Terms like "circle," "loom," "board," or "flower"
- No product or service involved - just money changing hands

Real-World Examples

"Susu" scams: A traditional rotating savings practice twisted into illegal schemes.

Blessing Loom scams on Facebook (2020): Went viral during COVID-19 lockdowns, then collapsed within weeks.

CashApp gifting schemes: Circulated widely on social media, often targeting younger users and the financially vulnerable.

How to Protect Yourself

If you must recruit others to earn, it's a scam.

Don't fall for social pressure from friends or family already involved.

Report gifting schemes to consumer protection authorities. They're illegal in many countries.

Educate others. Many people unknowingly promote these, thinking they're helping.

Remember: True generosity doesn't require a buy-in.

Consumer & Online Shopping Scams

- **Phishing Emails & Texts**

Trick users into giving personal/financial info.

- **Fake E-commerce Stores**

Collect payment, deliver nothing or counterfeit goods.

- **Product Review Scams**

Paying for fake reviews or “free trial” traps.

- **Overpayment Scams**

Scammer sends too much money, asks for refund, original payment bounces.

- **Online Marketplace Scams (Craigslist, Facebook)**

Fake listings, fake buyers/sellers.

- **Subscription Traps**

Free trial leads to ongoing hidden charges.

- **Dropshipping Scams**

Unethical operators that never deliver or use stolen images.

- **Fake Tech Support**

Posing as Microsoft/Apple to “fix” non-existent issues.

Phishing Emails & Texts: Hooking You with Fake Urgency

What Is Phishing?

Phishing is a type of scam where cybercriminals impersonate trusted companies or contacts (usually through emails or text messages) to trick you into revealing personal, financial, or login information. The goal? Steal your identity, access your accounts, or drain your bank.

How It Works

1. The Message

® You receive an email or text pretending to be from:

- Your bank
- A major retailer (Amazon, PayPal, Apple)
- Government agencies (IRS, HMRC, etc.)
- Delivery companies (FedEx, DHL)

2. The Bait

® The message may say:

- "Your account has been locked. Verify now."
- "You've won a prize! Claim it here."
- "Suspicious login attempt. Reset your password."

3. The Hook

® You're given a link to click or a form to fill out.

® The fake site looks almost identical to the real one.

® Once you enter your data, it goes straight to the scammer.

4. The Damage

® Stolen login credentials are used to access:

- Bank accounts
- Shopping sites
- Email (for further scams)

® Or your identity is sold on the dark web.

Variants of Phishing

- Spear Phishing: Personalized messages targeting you specifically.
- Smishing: Phishing via SMS/text message.
- Vishing: Voice phishing via phone calls.
- Business Email Compromise: Impersonating your boss or coworkers in professional settings.

Red Flags to Watch For

- Urgent or threatening tone: “Immediate action required!”
- Suspicious email address or misspelled domains (e.g., amaz0n.com)
- Generic greetings: “Dear customer” instead of your name
- Links that don’t match the official website
- §Attachments you weren’t expecting

Real-World Examples

PayPal phishing emails: Fake login alerts tricking users into giving up account info.

IRS/Tax scams: Claiming you owe taxes or are due a refund.

Delivery phishing: Fake tracking links or failed delivery notices (especially around holidays).

How to Protect Yourself

Never click suspicious links, go to the site manually.

Check the sender's email carefully.

Use two-factor authentication on your accounts.

Keep your software and antivirus up to date.

Report phishing to the real company or your government's cybersecurity agency.

Fake E-commerce Stores: When "Too Good to Be True" Really Is

What Are Fake Online Stores?

Fake e-commerce websites look like real online shops, but they're designed purely to steal your money, data, or both. These sites lure shoppers with unbelievably low prices, slick designs, and fake reviews. After you place an order, one of three things happens:

- You receive nothing
- You get a counterfeit or junk item
- Or your credit card is stolen

How It Works

1. The Setup

® Scammers build a website (or social media page) that mimics a legit store.

® They often use:

- Stolen product photos
- AI-generated reviews
- Fake trust seals (like Norton or PayPal verified badges)

2. The Bait

® You're enticed by:

- 80% off designer items
- Clearance sales that end "tonight"
- Free shipping on all orders
- Hard-to-find gadgets at a fraction of the price

3. The Transaction

® You place an order and pay with a credit card or PayPal.

® You get an order confirmation, but nothing ever arrives.

® Or you get a cheap knockoff worth pennies.

4. The Aftermath

® The site vanishes or stops responding.

® Your personal data may be used for identity theft or sold online.

® You might also be enrolled in unwanted subscriptions or receive fraudulent charges.

Common Variants

- Clone Stores: Look exactly like a real brand's site (e.g., nikeoutlet-clearance.com).
- Instagram Ads: Directing you to shady sites that disappear after a few weeks.
- Pop-Up Seasonal Sites: Appear during holidays or events (Black Friday, Christmas), then disappear.
- "Brand Ambassadors Wanted": You're offered free products, just pay shipping (and never receive anything).

Red Flags to Watch For

- Deals that seem too good to be true
- Poor grammar or strange URLs
- No contact info, physical address, or return policy
- Only payment options are crypto, wire transfer, or gift cards
- Domain is newly created

Real-World Examples

Romwe & Shein copycats: Fake fashion sites using stolen images from fast fashion brands.

Tech gadget scams: Wireless earbuds, drones, or smartwatches advertised for $10–$20.

Covid-era PPE scams: Fake websites sold masks and sanitizer but delivered nothing.

How to Protect Yourself

Google the store name + "scam" before buying.

Stick to known retailers or marketplaces with buyer protection.

Check reviews on independent sites (not just on their page).

Use a credit card, not a debit card, for online purchases.

Avoid clicking on ads. Search for the product manually instead.

Product Review Scams: When 5 Stars = 100% Lies

What Are Product Review Scams?

Product review scams are deceptive practices where sellers manipulate online reviews to boost their product's image, or bury their competitors. This creates a false sense of trust, leading people to spend money on low-quality, fake, or even dangerous products.

Some scams also involve "free trials" that come with hidden subscriptions, where you're tricked into giving glowing reviews in exchange for a so-called deal.

How It Works

1. The Setup

® A product appears with hundreds or thousands of 5-star reviews.
® It looks like a best-seller, with glowing testimonials, photos, and even video reviews.

2. The Reality

® Most reviews are:

- Paid for
- Written by bots
- Left in exchange for free products

® Some sellers use review hijacking, where good reviews from a different product are transferred to a bad one.

3. The Free Trial Trap

® You're offered a "free" product in exchange for a review.
® You give your credit card "for shipping", only to be charged monthly for a subscription.
® In some cases, you're required to leave a 5-star review before the product is even shipped.

Common Variants

- Amazon review rings: Groups that mass-produce fake reviews across multiple accounts.
- Facebook group scams: Users are offered full product refunds after they leave a 5-star review.
- Review bots: AI-written praise flooding listings in minutes.
- "As seen on TV" free trials: Hidden in the fine print are auto-renewal fees and zero refunds.

Red Flags to Watch For

- Hundreds of nearly identical reviews posted on the same day
- Over-the-top language ("This changed my life!!!")
- Reviews with poor grammar or unnatural phrasing
- No mention of negatives, every review is 5 stars
- Too many photos that look staged or professionally taken
- "Sponsored" or incentivized review disclosure missing

Real-World Examples

Amazon banned over 600 Chinese brands for fake review practices.

Trustpilot abuse: Some companies were caught paying users for 5-star ratings while reporting or hiding negative ones.

Free keto pills trial: Users gave glowing reviews to get "free" bottles - then got stuck with auto-charges they couldn't cancel.

How to Protect Yourself

Use review analyzer tools (like Fakespot or ReviewMeta) to scan for suspicious reviews.

Sort by 1-star reviews to see what people are really saying.

Beware of "free trial" reviews. They're often part of a larger scam.

Avoid sellers that request reviews before delivery.

Buy from verified sellers, not new or unknown vendors with perfect ratings.

Overpayment Scams: When Getting Paid Ends Up Costing You

What Are Overpayment Scams?

In an overpayment scam, the scammer pretends to be a buyer (or sometimes a client or employer) and sends you more money than agreed: often by check, bank transfer, or PayPal. They'll then ask you to send the extra back, only for you to find out later that their original payment was fake or fraudulent.

By the time the bank catches the fraud, you're out the money you sent back (and possibly your item or service, too).

How It Works

1. The Offer

® You're selling something online (e.g., on Craigslist, eBay, Facebook Marketplace).
® A buyer quickly agrees to purchase it, often sight unseen.

2. The "Accidental" Overpayment

® They "accidentally" send you too much money:

- "Oops! I added an extra zero."
- "I also sent you money for the shipper, can you pass it on to them?"

® You may receive a check or notification from PayPal/Zelle/Venmo.

3. The Refund Request

® They'll urgently ask you to return the difference: often via bank transfer, gift card, or a payment app.
® You comply, thinking you're doing the right thing.

4. The Sting

® Their original payment bounces or is flagged as fake days later.
® Your bank reverses the deposit, but the money you "refunded" is already gone.

Common Variants

- Freelancer job scams: "Client" sends overpaid check, then ghosts after asking for the extra to be sent back.
- Pet buyer scams: Someone pays extra to ship a pet, asks you to send the "shipping fee" to a third party.
- Fake PayPal emails: You're tricked into thinking funds were sent, but it's just a spoofed notification.
- Mystery shopper scams: You're asked to buy gift cards with part of a check - then the check bounces.

Red Flags to Watch For

- Buyer insists on paying by check or money order
- They overpay "by accident" or include extra for a "shipping agent"
- They push for a quick refund of the difference
- You receive unexpected funds via digital wallet
- You're asked to send money, gift cards, or crypto back

Real-World Examples

Craigslist car sales: Scammers send fake cashier's checks with shipping included, then ask for the balance back.

Freelance job boards: Fraudulent clients overpay for services, then vanish after getting partial refunds.

College housing scams: "Roommate" overpays rent, asks for the extra back, then their payment is reversed.

How to Protect Yourself

Never refund "accidental" overpayments. Insist on canceling and resending the correct amount.

Wait for checks to fully clear (can take up to 10 business days).

Use secure payment platforms with buyer/seller protections.

Don't accept overpayments from strangers, especially if they insist on urgency.

Verify payment confirmations independently, not just via email or screenshots.

Online Marketplace Scams: The Danger Behind "Local Deals"

What Are Online Marketplace Scams?

Online marketplaces like Craigslist, Facebook Marketplace, OfferUp, and Gumtree are meant for peer-to-peer buying and selling. But scammers love these platforms because there's no buyer protection, limited verification, and a steady stream of trusting users. Scams come from both fake buyers and fake sellers, and they can cost you money, products, or even put your safety at risk.

How It Works

Fake Sellers

1. Post attractive items (iPhones, cars, appliances) for very low prices.
2. Claim they're moving, in the military, or have to sell quickly.
3. Ask for payment upfront, usually through Zelle, PayPal, Venmo, or gift cards.
4. Once you send the money, the seller vanishes and no product is ever delivered.

Fake Buyers

1. Agree to purchase your item, often without negotiating.
2. Suggest overpayment (see previous scam), ask for "courier" fees, or want to pay via shady methods.
3. Sometimes, they send a fraudulent check or fake PayPal/Zelle confirmation.
4. You lose your item or money, or get caught in a refund scam.

Common Variants

- Fake apartment listings: Renters are asked for deposits before seeing the place.
- Ticket scams: Fake event tickets sold for popular concerts or sports games.
- Job equipment scams: You're hired remotely and asked to buy “required gear” from a fake vendor.
- Scammer courier scam: Someone offers to send a courier for your item - after you pay a shipping fee.

Red Flags to Watch For

- Buyer or seller refuses to meet in person (or insists on it under suspicious circumstances).
- Asking for payment via gift cards, crypto, wire transfers, or prepaid debit cards.
- The listing sounds too good to be true: brand-new iPhone for $200, for example.
- Excuses like: "I'm overseas," "I'm buying for my cousin," or "I'll have a mover pick it up."
- Communication only happens via email or WhatsApp, not on the platform itself.

Real-World Examples

Facebook Marketplace pet scams: Puppies "for sale" that never existed.

Craigslist car scams: Non-existent vehicles sold with fake shipping services.

Fake event ticket resales: Users pay for e-tickets that get flagged as invalid at the door.

How to Protect Yourself

Meet in person, in public, ideally at a police station parking lot (many are designated for this purpose).

....

Never pay in advance, pay only after verifying the product in person.

....

Avoid strange payment methods. Stick to cash or secure app transfers during the meetup.

....

Trust your instincts. If it feels off, walk away.

....

Report scammers to the platform immediately.

Subscription Traps: When “Free” Ends Up Costing You Monthly

What Are Subscription Traps?

Subscription traps start with a tempting offer: a “free trial,” “just pay shipping,” or “limited-time access” to a product or service. What many don’t realize is that hidden in the fine print is a recurring subscription, often with difficult cancellation policies, hidden fees, or unreachable customer service. Victims often don’t notice until multiple charges hit their account.

How It Works

1. The Bait

® You see a product promoted as:

- "Risk-free trial"
- "Only pay $1 for shipping!"
- "One-month free access, cancel anytime"

2. The Hook

® You enter your credit card for the "free" offer.

® Buried in small text (or not at all), you've actually agreed to a recurring monthly charge - often $40, $80, or more.

3. The Trap

® After a short trial (sometimes only 3–5 days), you're billed automatically.

® Attempts to cancel are met with:

- No phone number
- Fake customer support
- "You didn't meet cancellation terms"
- Or they simply keep charging you anyway

Common Variants

- Health & beauty scams: Anti-aging creams, keto pills, CBD oils, or muscle enhancers.
- Digital subscriptions: Horoscope apps, dating services, VPNs, or PC optimization tools.
- Celebrity-endorsed offers: Scammers use fake ads with celebrities like Oprah, Elon Musk, or Shark Tank judges to lure you in.
- "Win a free gift" traps: You're told you've won - but must claim it by signing up for a service.

Red Flags to Watch For

- “Free trial” requires a credit card
- No clear explanation of ongoing costs
- You can't find contact or cancellation info easily
- Terms are vague, hidden, or written in light gray text
- The product is marketed with fake celebrity endorsements
- The trial period is very short, sometimes only a few days

Real-World Examples

“Keto pill” scams: Users thought they were buying a one-time bottle. Got stuck with $90/month auto-billing.

Skin cream offers: Consumers billed monthly even after sending the product back.

Streaming app traps: Users signed up through fake “download now” buttons and were charged monthly.

How to Protect Yourself

Never enter card info for a free offer unless the company is reputable and the terms are clear.

Read the fine print carefully - especially the Terms of Service and Return Policy.

Use virtual or disposable credit cards when testing new services.

Check your bank statements regularly for small recurring charges.

Cancel immediately after ordering if you change your mind.

Report abuses to your bank and relevant consumer protection agencies.

Dropshipping Scams: The Mirage Behind the "Great Deal"

What Are Dropshipping Scams?

Dropshipping is a legitimate e-commerce model where sellers list products they don't physically stock: when a customer buys, the seller forwards the order to a supplier who ships it directly. But scammers exploit this model by creating shady online stores with exaggerated claims, fake urgency, or stolen product photos. Many buyers end up receiving cheap knockoffs, massive delays, or nothing at all.

How It Works

1. The Tempting Deal

® You see an ad (usually on Instagram, TikTok, or Facebook) for a "limited-time" or deeply discounted product.
® The store looks polished, and the product may have viral appeal (e.g., "smartwatch for $10!").

2. The Purchase

® You order and pay with your card or PayPal.
® You may get a confirmation email, but no tracking or delayed shipping updates.

3. The Disappointment

® The item never arrives, or:

- It takes 4–8 weeks, coming directly from China.
- It's a cheap, unusable knockoff of what was advertised.

® Customer support either ignores you, gives vague excuses, or blames "shipping issues."

4. The Exit

® The website vanishes weeks later, often replaced by another clone.

Common Variants

- Impulse-buy gadgets: Neck massagers, posture correctors, mini printers.
- Pet accessories: Glowing collars, “pet translator” buttons.
- “Just pay shipping” scams: Claiming the item is free, but you pay a high shipping fee and get junk (or nothing).
- Fake influencer stores: Claiming a celebrity or influencer brand is behind it, when it’s not.

Red Flags to Watch For

- Products that seem too cheap to be real
- No clear information on shipping times, refunds, or physical business address
- Excessive use of "only 5 left!" or countdown timers
- Reviews that look too positive or generic
- Heavily advertised via social media influencers or meme pages
- No brand reputation or presence outside of one website

Real-World Examples

“StarScope Monocular” scam: Promised military-grade optics; delivered dollar-store toy lenses.

TikTok ring light stores: Advertised trendy gadgets, but delivered broken or counterfeit items - or nothing.

Shady fitness gear ads: Equipment shown in high-quality videos turns out to be tiny, flimsy, and unusable.

How to Protect Yourself

Check reviews on independent sites, not just on the seller's page.

Look up the store name with keywords like "scam" or "complaints."

Avoid sites that only offer one product, especially with no company info.

Use trusted marketplaces (Amazon, Etsy) instead of random Instagram stores.

Pay with PayPal or credit cards that offer buyer protection, never Zelle, Venmo, or crypto.

Fake Tech Support Scams: The Fix That Breaks Your Bank

What Are Fake Tech Support Scams?

Fake tech support scams trick you into believing your computer has a virus or technical issue. Then scammers pose as legitimate companies (like Microsoft, Apple, or antivirus providers) to “help” you. In reality, they’re stealing your money, data, or remote access. These scams often target older adults, but anyone can fall for them, especially when they come with urgent warnings.

How It Works

1. The Scare Tactic

® You get:

- A pop-up warning while browsing
- A cold call pretending to be from Microsoft/Apple
- A fake email saying your device is compromised

® It tells you to call a number immediately or click to fix it

2. The Fake Help

® A scammer answers, claiming to be from tech support.

® They may ask you to install remote access software like TeamViewer or AnyDesk.

® They show you fake “error logs” to scare you further.

3. The Damage

® They:

- Charge you hundreds for fake services
- Install spyware or malware
- Access your banking info or files

® If you allow remote access, they might lock you out of your device or hold it hostage for ransom.

Common Variants

- Browser lock scams: Your screen freezes with an alert saying "Call Microsoft immediately."
- Refund scams: Scammer says you're owed a refund, but "accidentally" overpays you. Then demands you send the difference.
- Fake antivirus renewals: You get an email or call saying your subscription to Norton, McAfee, etc. is auto-renewing for $399.
- Imposter techs: They call pretending to have detected "suspicious activity" on your account.

Red Flags to Watch For

- Sudden pop-ups that lock your browser with scary warnings
- Unsolicited phone calls claiming to be from Microsoft, Apple, Norton, etc.
- Anyone asking for remote access to your computer
- You're told to pay in gift cards, wire transfers, or crypto
- High-pressure tactics: "If you don't act now, you'll lose everything"

Real-World Examples

"Microsoft tech support" pop-up: Claimed the user had a virus. Charged $500 for "removal" and stole credit card info.

Norton fake renewal email: Victim called the number, gave remote access, and was locked out of their banking app.

Elderly victim case: Lost $2,800 after allowing "Apple support" to remotely access their MacBook.

How to Protect Yourself

Never call numbers from pop-ups. Real tech companies do not display phone numbers like that.

If in doubt, close your browser or shut down your device.

Use reputable antivirus and ad-blockers to avoid malicious pop-ups.

Don't trust unsolicited phone calls claiming to be from support.

If you did give access, disconnect your internet immediately, run a virus scan, and contact your bank if personal info was exposed.

Relationship & Emotional Manipulation Scams

- **Romance Scams**

Long-distance "lovers" who eventually ask for money.

- **Catfishing**

Fake identities used to exploit someone emotionally and/or financially.

- **"Sugar Daddy" Scams**

Fake benefactor asks for upfront "processing" fees.

- **Military Romance Scams**

Impersonating soldiers needing financial help.

Romance Scams: When Love Is Just a Lie

What Are Romance Scams?

Romance scams target people looking for emotional connection: on dating sites, apps, or even social media. The scammer pretends to build a genuine romantic relationship, often over weeks or months. Once trust is earned, they fabricate a crisis or opportunity that requires you to send money. These scams are emotionally devastating and financially crippling, especially because the victim believes they're helping someone they love.

How It Works

1. The Approach

® You're contacted on a dating app, Facebook, Instagram, or even LinkedIn.
® They have a flawless profile photo, charming personality, and seem deeply interested in you.

2. The Relationship

® They build trust through long chats, frequent compliments, and emotional intimacy.
® They may say they live far away: deployed overseas, working on an oil rig, or in another country.

3. The Ask

® After trust is built, they mention a crisis:

- Medical emergency
- Travel issues
- Inheritance problem
- Business investment opportunity

® They ask you to send money - often starting small and growing larger.

4. The Vanish

® Once they've drained as much as possible, they disappear.
® Or they may try to keep it going by inventing new emergencies.

Common Variants

- Crypto twist: Scammer “lover” claims to help you invest in crypto. Then steals everything.
- Visa or travel fee scam: They want to come visit but need money for tickets, visas, or fake taxes.
- Romance blackmail: After gaining intimate photos, they threaten to release them unless paid.

Red Flags to Watch For

- They say “I love you” too quickly
- They avoid video calls or in-person meetings
- They claim to be traveling or working in remote areas
- They make financial requests, no matter how small
- They ask for unusual payment methods: crypto, gift cards, wire transfers

Real-World Examples

A woman in the U.S. lost $300,000 to a man she believed was a doctor working in Syria.

An elderly man sent over $70,000 to a woman who claimed she was stranded in Eastern Europe.

During the pandemic, romance scams spiked as scammers took advantage of isolation and loneliness.

How to Protect Yourself

Never send money to someone you haven't met in person.

Do a reverse image search of their profile picture to check for stolen identities.

Keep conversations on the dating platform as long as possible. Moving to private apps is often a red flag.

Be skeptical of anyone who refuses video chats or always has excuses not to meet.

Talk to friends or family about your new relationship. Outside perspective helps.

Catfishing: The Fake Identity Behind the Screen

What Is Catfishing?

Catfishing is when someone creates a false online identity, often using fake photos, names, and backstories to deceive others, usually for emotional manipulation, revenge, or financial gain. While not always about money, many catfishers evolve their scams into romance frauds, blackmail, or even elaborate schemes targeting the vulnerable or lonely.

How It Works

1. The Fake Profile

® They use stolen or AI-generated photos to create an attractive persona.

® Profiles are usually too perfect: model-like pictures, impressive careers, exotic locations.

2. The Emotional Hook

® They message you on dating apps, Facebook, Instagram, or even games/chat forums.

® They form a deep, emotional bond (sometimes over months) by mirroring your interests, telling you what you want to hear, and being available 24/7.

3. The Lie Grows

® They always have excuses not to video chat or meet (bad camera, traveling, sick, military duty).

® As the relationship deepens, they may ask for money, gifts, or personal favors - or use your emotions to manipulate you into helping them in other ways.

4. The Crash

® Some catfishers disappear after getting what they want.

® Others keep the illusion alive indefinitely, or even blackmail the victim with private photos or conversations.

Common Variants

- Revenge catfishing: Ex-partners or enemies pretend to be someone else to emotionally toy with or humiliate the victim.
- Troll catfishing: Internet trolls catfish for fun, trying to waste your time or cause embarrassment.
- Social experimenters: Some catfishers claim they're “testing” people or doing it out of boredom or loneliness.
- Business catfishing: Posing as CEOs, recruiters, or investors to lure professionals into scams.

Red Flags to Watch For

- Refuses to video chat or meet in person
- Their photos look too professional or glamorous
- Their life seems too dramatic: constantly in crises, traveling, or emotionally extreme
- They avoid detailed questions about themselves or give inconsistent stories
- They try to move the conversation off-platform quickly (to WhatsApp, Telegram, etc.)
- They ask for money, nudes, or sensitive information

Real-World Examples

A woman discovered her "boyfriend" of 2 years was actually a middle-aged neighbor using fake male photos.

A teenage girl was tricked into sending private photos to someone pretending to be a modeling agent - who turned out to be a classmate.

A U.S. man lost his job after being lured by a fake company created by a catfish who used stolen corporate branding.

How to Protect Yourself

Do reverse image searches of profile pictures on Google or TinEye.

Ask for a real-time video call, not just photos or pre-recorded clips.

Be cautious if they avoid sharing real social media accounts or have minimal history.

Never send money, nudes, or personal data to someone you haven't met in person.

If you suspect a catfish, cut contact immediately and report the profile to the platform.

“Sugar Daddy” Scams: Easy Money That Comes at a Cost

What Are “Sugar Daddy” Scams?

In a legitimate sugar relationship, one person (the “sugar daddy” or “sugar mommy”) offers financial support to another (the “sugar baby”) in exchange for companionship, attention, or arrangement-based interaction. But scammers exploit this idea by pretending to be wealthy benefactors (offering quick money, gifts, or allowances) only to turn it into a fraudulent trap that costs the victim money instead.

How It Works

1. The Offer

® You're contacted on Instagram, Snapchat, TikTok, dating apps, or even via random DMs.
® They say things like:

- "I want to spoil you"
- "Looking for someone to send $500 weekly"
- "No meetups necessary, just want good company"

2. The Hook

® Once you express interest, they ask for your bank info, Cash App, PayPal, or Venmo.
® They may even show you fake payment receipts or screenshots of big transactions.

3. The Trap

® Then comes the catch: they say there's a "processing fee", bank limit issue, or security requirement.
® They ask you to pay a small fee first to release the full payment, usually through gift cards, crypto, or money apps.
® You pay... and the promised "allowance" never arrives.

4. The Repeat (or Threat)

® Some scammers repeat the process with more excuses.
® Others may threaten to expose chats or photos if you don't send more money.

Common Variants

- Fake payment reversals: They "accidentally" send too much and ask you to refund the difference. Then their original transfer bounces.
- Crypto sugar scams: They say they'll invest your money for you, then vanish.
- Check fraud version: They mail a check that looks legit, ask you to withdraw and forward part of it - only for the check to bounce days later.

Red Flags to Watch For

- Offers of large payments for little to no interaction
- Requests for upfront fees, regardless of the reason
- Use of gift cards, crypto, or sketchy payment methods
- Poor grammar or overly generic language ("I want to spoil you real good")
- Refusal to video chat or verify their identity
- Profile photos that look like models or stock images

Real-World Examples

A college student lost over $1,200 after paying "clearance fees" to a fake sugar daddy who never delivered.

Victims have reported receiving fake screenshots of PayPal transfers to build trust before the scam.

An 18-year-old was blackmailed after sharing personal information with someone posing as a sugar mommy.

How to Protect Yourself

If someone offers to pay you for doing nothing, it's probably a scam.

Never pay any fees upfront to receive money. Real sugar arrangements don't work that way.

Be skeptical of anyone who avoids video calls or sharing real profiles.

Use anonymous usernames and don't share banking info with strangers.

Report suspicious messages to the platform. These scams violate terms of service.

Military Romance Scams: Stolen Valor, Stolen Money

What Are Military Romance Scams?

Military romance scams involve scammers who pretend to be active-duty soldiers, officers, or veterans, often stationed overseas. They exploit the trust, respect, and patriotism people associate with the military to build emotional connections and eventually ask for money under false pretenses. These scams are especially cruel because they use fake stories of hardship, service, and sacrifice to manipulate victims.

How It Works

1. The Setup

® You're contacted by someone claiming to be in the U.S. military (or from another country's armed forces).
® Their profile includes military uniforms, medals, and heroic-sounding bios - often with stolen photos from real soldiers.

2. The Relationship

® They strike up a romance quickly, saying things like:
- "You're the only one who makes me feel normal again."
- "It's hard being deployed, but you're keeping me going."

® They may claim to be in combat zones, secret missions, or remote bases where communication is limited.

3. The Ask

® Once trust is established, they say they need money for:
- Travel home
- Medical care
- Leave papers or early discharge
- Communication fees
- Customs clearance for a package

® They might say their military pay is delayed or inaccessible while deployed.

4. The Collapse

® Victims may send thousands of dollars before realizing it's all fake.
® The scammer may disappear, or keep asking for more money until the victim is financially and emotionally drained.

Common Variants

- "Package delivery" scam: They claim to have sent you a valuable package (like gold, cash, or documents), but you need to pay a customs fee or release fee.
- Fake military email addresses: They use lookalike military emails (e.g., ".mil-service@mail.com") to seem legitimate.
- Fake officials: Someone posing as a general, embassy staff, or customs agent may message you, demanding fees or paperwork.

Red Flags to Watch For

- Says they can't video call due to military restrictions (this is false).
- Requests money for travel, communication, or leave documents.
- Stories involve combat injuries, secret missions, or dramatic hardship.
- Their military photos look overly polished or suspiciously generic.
- Asks for payment via gift cards, crypto, wire transfers, or apps like Zelle or Cash App.

Real-World Examples

A woman in the UK lost £240,000 to a scammer claiming to be a U.S. soldier stuck in Syria.

The U.S. Army has reported that real soldiers' photos are constantly stolen to fuel these scams.

Some scams have multiple actors, including fake "military lawyers" or "generals" demanding payment to "authorize" the soldier's leave.

How to Protect Yourself

Never send money to someone claiming to be a soldier online.

Know that real military personnel do not need help paying for leave, travel, or phone access.

Reverse-search photos used in profiles to see if they've been used in other scams.

Be wary of romantic connections that develop very quickly or feel emotionally intense.

Report the scam to the appropriate authorities and dating platform.

Housing & Real Estate Scams

- **Rental Scams**

Fake listings requiring deposits before viewing.

- **Foreclosure Relief Scams**

Targeting desperate homeowners with false promises.

- **Property Title Fraud**

Transferring ownership via forged documents.

Rental Scams: The Home You'll Never Move Into

What Are Rental Scams?

Rental scams trick people - usually renters - into paying deposits or rent for properties that don't exist, aren't available, or aren't owned by the scammer. These scams often prey on people in urgent need of housing, especially in competitive markets or during moves.

How It Works

1. The Fake Listing

® Scammers copy real property listings from websites like Zillow, Craigslist, Facebook Marketplace, or rental apps.
® They may list unavailable properties at unusually low prices to draw attention.
® The contact info is changed to route inquiries directly to the scammer.

2. The Emotional Pressure

® The scammer responds quickly, sometimes claiming they're out of town, traveling for work, or stationed overseas.
® They push for a quick deal, saying things like:

- "Many people are interested, first to pay gets it."
- "We can't do in-person tours, but I'll mail you the keys once payment is received."

3. The Payment Trap

® Victims are asked to pay a security deposit, first month's rent, or application fee upfront.
® Payment is requested through wire transfer, Cash App, Zelle, Venmo, or even cryptocurrency.
® After payment, the scammer disappears. No keys, no property, no refund.

Common Variants

- Vacation rental scams: Fake Airbnb or short-term rentals where the scammer pretends to be the host.
- Roommate scams: Someone pretends to need a roommate and asks for upfront rent or deposit.
- Fake landlords: Scammers show vacant homes they don't own and collect applications and fees from multiple victims.

Red Flags to Watch For

- Rent is "too good to be true" for the neighborhood.
- Landlord won't meet in person or show the property.
- Requests money before seeing the property.
- Excuses like "I'm out of the country" or "I'll mail the keys."
- Pressure to act quickly or lose the deal.
- Payment methods that are untraceable (gift cards, crypto, wire transfer).

Real-World Examples

A college student paid $1,200 for an apartment deposit only to find out the listing was stolen and already rented to someone else.

A scammer posted photos of a luxury condo (stolen from Zillow), collected deposits from multiple victims, and vanished.

One case involved scammers showing victims a real property they'd broken into, then taking deposits and disappearing before the lease was signed.

How to Protect Yourself

Never send money without seeing the property in person.

Verify ownership through public property records or local housing registries.

Look up the address online to see if it's listed multiple times (a sign it was copied).

Use reputable rental platforms that offer protections and verified hosts.

If it feels rushed or suspicious, walk away. Legitimate landlords won’t pressure you into payment before a viewing.

Foreclosure Relief Scams: False Hope for Desperate Homeowners

What Are Foreclosure Relief Scams?

These scams target homeowners who are behind on mortgage payments or facing foreclosure. Scammers pretend to be financial experts, legal advisors, or government-affiliated organizations offering to "save" your home. But their real goal is to take your money, your personal info, or even your home itself.

How It Works

1. The Approach

® Scammers often obtain public foreclosure records and target those in financial distress.
® They reach out via mail, phone calls, door-to-door visits, or even ads online.
® The pitch: “We’ll stop the foreclosure,” “We can negotiate with your lender,” or “We’ll buy your house and rent it back to you.”

2. The False Promises

® They offer loan modifications, refinancing help, or legal assistance - but require upfront fees, sometimes thousands of dollars.
® They might also convince you to sign over your deed as part of a “temporary transfer” to help with negotiations.

3. The Outcome

® After receiving your payment, they disappear or string you along with no real progress.
® In the worst cases, homeowners unknowingly sign over ownership of their home and are evicted later.

Common Variants

- “Forensic audits”: They promise to find errors in your mortgage documents that will get the loan canceled - for a hefty fee.
- Rent-back scams: The scammer buys your home “temporarily” and lets you stay as a tenant, then evicts you and keeps the property.
- Fake nonprofit or government aid: They impersonate HUD counselors, use official-looking documents, and claim to be affiliated with federal relief programs.

Red Flags to Watch For

- You're asked to pay upfront for help.
- They guarantee they can stop foreclosure or get your loan modified.
- Pressure to sign documents quickly, without reading.
- Told to stop communicating with your lender.
- Offered to sign over the deed temporarily as part of the solution.
- Use of vague business names or refusal to provide proper identification.

Real-World Examples

A family paid over $3,500 to a “foreclosure expert” who promised to delay the bank’s action. Nothing was done, and they lost the home.

One scam used HUD logos on fake documents and set up a toll-free number to appear official.

Several scams involved "trust agreements" where homeowners lost their titles after being misled about legal documents.

How to Protect Yourself

Don't pay upfront fees. It's illegal in many countries for foreclosure assistance services to require payment before delivering results.

Work only with certified housing counselors approved by your government (e.g., HUD-approved in the U.S.).

Never sign over your deed unless you're selling the house through a trusted, verified process.

Contact your lender directly. They're often more willing to work with you than you think.

Always read the fine print and get a second opinion from a legal or financial professional before signing anything.

Property Title Fraud: When Your Home Is Stolen on Paper

What Is Property Title Fraud?

Property title fraud occurs when a scammer illegally transfers ownership of your property to themselves or someone else using forged documents. In many cases, the victim doesn't even realize their home has been stolen until they receive a foreclosure notice, see a "For Sale" sign, or are evicted from a property they still legally believe they own.

How It Works

1. Identity Theft

® Scammers gather personal information about a property owner, especially absentee landlords, the elderly, or owners of vacant homes.
® They forge documents using fake IDs, notary stamps, or altered deeds.

2. Filing the Paperwork

® The forged deed is submitted to the local land registry or title office, which often has little to no verification checks.
® The fraudster now appears as the legal owner of the property on paper.

3. Monetizing the Theft

® The scammer might:

- Sell the home to an unsuspecting buyer.
- Take out a mortgage or line of credit against the property.
- Rent it out to tenants.
- Evict the rightful owner through legal trickery.

4. The Victim Finds Out Too Late

® Many victims don't know anything's wrong until they try to refinance, sell, or get hit with foreclosure proceedings on loans they never took.

Common Variants

- Deed theft targeting the elderly: Scammers pose as helpers or "investors" and trick owners into signing over their property.
- Vacant home scams: Properties with no occupants are quietly stolen and mortgaged.
- Fake heirs: In inheritance cases, fraudsters pretend to be the rightful inheritor and claim ownership of estates.

Red Flags to Watch For

- You stop receiving property tax bills or utility notices.
- You receive mortgage documents for a loan you never applied for.
- Someone is living in or showing your home without your consent.
- You see unexplained activity on your property title or deed.
- You're denied a loan or refinance due to a lien or mortgage you didn't know about.

Real-World Examples

A Brooklyn woman returned to find her paid-off home was "sold" without her knowledge. The scammer forged documents and fled.

A Detroit homeowner lost her title when a fraudster filed a forged quitclaim deed and flipped the house to a third party.

Criminals in some cases have taken multiple mortgages out on a property they didn't own, leaving the rightful owner buried in legal issues.

How to Protect Yourself

Regularly check your property records with your local title office or land registry.

Consider title insurance that covers fraud-related loss.

Set up alerts if your registry offers notifications for changes to property records.

Be especially cautious if you:

- Own a second/vacant home.
- Are an elderly homeowner.
- Live out of state or abroad.

Report suspected fraud immediately to:

- Your county recorder's office
- Law enforcement
- A real estate attorney

Employment & Business Scams

- **Work-from-Home Scams**

Fake jobs requiring upfront payments for training/tools.

- **Mystery Shopper Scams**

Asking you to cash checks and "evaluate" stores.

- **Fake Resume Services**

Overcharging for low-quality or plagiarized resumes.

- **Invoice Scams**

Sending fake invoices to small businesses or startups.

- **MLM vs Pyramid Schemes**

Grey area where many "legit" MLMs border illegal structure.

Work-from-Home Scams: The Job That Pays Nothing but Costs You

What Are Work-from-Home Scams?

These scams target job seekers, especially those looking for remote or flexible work, by advertising fake job opportunities that promise high income from the comfort of home. The catch? You'll likely be asked to pay upfront for training, equipment, or certifications, and then either receive nothing or get stuck in an exploitative setup.

How It Works

1. The Attractive Job Listing

® Found on job boards, social media, or even sent by email.

® Promises things like:

- "Earn $500 a day working from home!"
- "No experience necessary!"
- "Flexible hours, guaranteed income!"

2. The Application & Hook

® After you "apply," the scammer contacts you quickly and offers you the job - often with no interview.

® You're told you need to pay upfront for:

- Training materials
- Background checks
- Starter kits
- Special software or tools

3. The Money Drain

® Once you pay, communication may go silent.

® Or you may be strung along with more requests for money.

® In some versions, they send you a fake check to buy equipment, and when it bounces, you're left responsible for the loss.

Common Variants

- Stuffing envelopes: Pay upfront for a "mailing job" that never pays.
- Virtual assistant roles: Fake employers offer high pay and ask you to buy supplies or pay fees upfront.
- Check scams: You're sent a check to buy gear, told to keep a portion, and wire the rest. Then the check bounces.
- Amazon/affiliate reshipping jobs: You're tricked into laundering goods or handling stolen merchandise.

Red Flags to Watch For

- Asked to pay money upfront for tools, training, or materials.
- Job offers with no interview or experience required.
- Ads filled with over-the-top promises ("Make $3,000 a week from your sofa!").
- Communication through personal email addresses, not company domains.
- The employer avoids video calls or live conversations.
- Poorly written job ads or vague job descriptions.

Real-World Examples

A stay-at-home parent lost over $1,000 to a fake transcription job that asked for software fees up front.

One scheme involved hiring people to "process payments", which turned out to be a money laundering operation.

Victims of envelope-stuffing jobs never received any materials or payment despite paying a “registration fee.”

How to Protect Yourself

Never pay to get a job. Real employers don't ask for upfront fees.

Research the company. Search for "[Company Name] + scam" online.

Only apply through trusted job platforms or the company's official website.

Be wary of unofficial communication, especially if sent from Gmail or Yahoo accounts.

If you receive a check, wait for it to fully clear (which can take weeks) before spending or sending any funds.

Trust your gut: If it seems too good to be true, it probably is.

Mystery Shopper Scams: A "Job" That Just Wants Your Bank Account

What Are Mystery Shopper Scams?

Mystery shopper scams impersonate legitimate customer service evaluation programs. Scammers lure people with offers to get paid to shop or dine at well-known stores or restaurants. But instead of evaluating businesses, victims are tricked into cashing fake checks or sharing personal and banking details, often resulting in financial loss.

How It Works

1. The Job Offer

® Victims receive an email, text, or letter offering a job as a “secret shopper” or “retail evaluator.”

® The offer sounds enticing: get paid to shop at places like Walmart, Target, or Starbucks.

® No experience required, and the promise of $200–$500 per assignment.

2. The Setup

® The scammer sends a fake check, usually for more than your "salary".

® You’re instructed to:

- Deposit the check.
- Use a portion to buy gift cards or make a wire transfer as part of your “evaluation.”
- Send the gift card codes or transfer receipt back as “evidence” of your visit.

3. The Sting

® A few days later, the check bounces, but your bank holds you responsible for the money.

® By then, you’ve already sent the real funds to the scammer, and they’re gone.

Common Variants

- Gift card audits: Told to buy gift cards, then send the codes "to verify the experience."
- Wire transfer testing: Instructed to send money via Western Union or MoneyGram as part of a "remittance quality check."
- ATM evaluation: Asked to withdraw and send back cash deposits "for security auditing."
- Overnight mailings: Scammers sometimes mail fake checks with impressive-looking documentation to appear legitimate.

Red Flags to Watch For

- You receive a check before doing any work.
- Asked to deposit and wire money or buy gift cards immediately.
- The sender uses free email services (Gmail, Yahoo) instead of company emails.
- No official application process, you're "hired" instantly.
- The job sounds too good to be true, and pays far too well for simple tasks.
- No real contact info or company website.

Real-World Examples

A college student received a $2,500 check with instructions to buy $1,800 in Apple gift cards. After sending the codes, the check bounced, and they owed the bank the full amount.

A retiree was tricked into wiring money through Western Union for a "customer service review." They lost over $3,000 and were never contacted again.

Some scams impersonate legitimate programs from real market research companies, making them harder to detect.

How to Protect Yourself

Never cash a check from someone you don't know and then send money back.

Real mystery shopping companies will never ask you to pay upfront or wire funds as part of an assignment.

Always verify with the Mystery Shopping Providers Association (MSPA) if the offer is real.

If it involves gift cards or wire transfers, it's a scam.

Report suspected scams to your local consumer protection agency or the Federal Trade Commission (FTC).

Fake Resume Services: Paying for a Shortcut That Leads Nowhere

What Are Fake Resume Services?

These scams prey on job seekers by offering resume writing, editing, or distribution services that promise to dramatically boost your chances of landing a job. In reality, many of these services are either overpriced, deliver plagiarized or low-quality content, or never deliver anything at all. Some even use the scam to harvest personal data.

How It Works

1. The Pitch

® You see ads online, get cold emails, or encounter social media posts offering professional resume help.
® Claims might include:
"Get hired 10x faster!"

- "Resumes written by former Fortune 500 recruiters!"
- "Guaranteed job placement within 30 days!"

2. The Payment

® You're asked to pay upfront fees, often ranging from $50 to $500 or more.
® Some services even offer "tiers," charging more for executive-level resumes or LinkedIn optimization.

3. The Letdown

® The resume you receive is often:

- Generic or plagiarized (copied from templates found online).
- Full of grammatical errors or written by someone without HR experience.
- Never delivered at all, despite full payment.

4. The Upsell or Exploit

® Scammers may try to sell you "job placement" add-ons, charge recurring fees, or ask for personal data under the guise of application assistance.
® In some cases, they may even resell your information to shady third parties or fake recruiters.

Common Variants

- Resume distribution scams: Claim to send your resume to "thousands of recruiters," but do nothing, or send it to spam inboxes.
- AI-written resume services that charge high prices for content generated by free tools.
- Fake recruiter outreach: Someone poses as a recruiter who insists your resume needs help, only to funnel you to their overpriced "resume expert."
- LinkedIn optimization scams that claim to "boost visibility" but just repaste your resume with buzzwords.

Red Flags to Watch For

- Guaranteed job offers or "interviews within days."
- Pressure to act fast with "limited-time offers."
- No way to verify the writers' credentials or portfolio.
- Overuse of buzzwords without specifics (e.g., "resume experts," "career coaches").
- Requests for sensitive personal info (SSN, full employment history, references) before any services are rendered.
- Poor spelling/grammar in the company's own marketing.

Real-World Examples

A job seeker paid $300 for a resume "written by former Google recruiters" but received a generic resume that was copy-pasted from online examples.

An overseas resume service collected payments but ghosted all customers after taking the money, leaving dozens without refunds or documentation.

A fake job board required resume uploads, which were then used to impersonate job seekers in identity theft schemes.

How to Protect Yourself

Use well-reviewed, reputable services with clear portfolios and customer feedback.

Search online for the service's name + "scam" or "reviews."

Ask for samples or credentials of the person who will be writing your resume.

Avoid any site that guarantees jobs or interview offers.

Consider local career centers, nonprofits, or university services, which often offer free or low-cost resume assistance.

Never provide sensitive information unless you've verified the company's legitimacy.

Invoice Scams: Fake Bills That Target Your Trust and Time

What Are Invoice Scams?

Invoice scams involve sending fraudulent bills or payment requests to individuals, small businesses, or startups in hopes they'll pay without realizing it's fake. These scams exploit busy environments, accounting confusion, or automated systems - relying on the assumption that not every charge is double-checked.

How It Works

1. The Fake Invoice Arrives

® A company receives a bill for something seemingly legitimate: office supplies, web hosting, domain renewal, software licenses, etc.

® It may appear to come from a known vendor, or a name that sounds familiar (like "WebHost Center Inc." or "Global Office Supplies").

2. Urgent Wording

® The invoice is labeled “past due”, or there’s a threat of service interruption.

® Some may include legal language or government-like formatting to increase urgency.

3. Payment Is Made

® An employee (or business owner) pays the invoice assuming it’s real.

® Later, they realize the product or service was never ordered, and the vendor doesn’t exist.

Common Variants

- Fake domain renewals: The bill warns your website will be shut down unless you "renew" immediately - usually at an inflated cost.
- Directory listing scams: A business is billed for being listed in a fake "online business directory."
- Office supply invoices: A bill for toner, printer paper, or tech support you never received.
- Government impersonation: Scammers pose as government agencies requiring business registration fees or compliance payments.
- Phishing hybrid: The invoice includes a link to "view your bill," which leads to a fake login page for Microsoft 365 or PayPal.

Red Flags to Watch For

- The invoice is unexpected and pressures immediate payment.
- No clear details about what the product or service actually is.
- Vendor names that are vague or slightly off from real ones.
- Contact info that doesn't match any existing business.
- Poor formatting, spelling mistakes, or generic company logos.
- Hyperlinks that go to suspicious or shortened URLs.

Real-World Examples

A small business received a bill for $399 to renew its domain. Thinking it was from their web host, they paid - only to later learn it was from a scammer.

Startups have been hit with fake invoices for "SEO services" or "compliance audits," only to find out they were never contracted.

Some scammers target dozens of businesses at once using mail merges to mass-produce invoices that look semi-customized.

How to Protect Yourself

Verify all invoices before payment, especially new or unfamiliar ones.

Train staff to question suspicious bills, especially under time pressure.

Keep a vendor approval list, and don't pay outside it without confirmation.

Match purchase orders to actual goods or services received.

Watch out for phishing links on e-invoices. Hover before clicking.

Report fake invoices to your local business fraud office or chamber of commerce.

MLM vs. Pyramid Schemes: The Thin Line Between Hustle and Fraud

What's the Difference?

Multilevel Marketing (MLM) companies and pyramid schemes often look very similar, but only one is technically legal. The key difference? Legitimate MLMs focus on selling real products, while pyramid schemes focus on recruitment over sales. Unfortunately, some MLMs blur the line so much, they function more like legalized scams than ethical businesses.

How It Works

1. The Recruitment Pitch

® Someone (often a friend or relative) approaches you with an "amazing business opportunity."
® You're told you can be your own boss, work from home, and earn passive income.
® You must buy a starter kit or inventory, often ranging from $100 to $5,000.

2. The Pressure to Recruit

® Earnings are heavily tied to bringing in more recruits, not product sales.
® You're promised bonuses, ranks, and commissions as your "downline" grows.

3. Product Sales (or the Illusion of It)

® Products may be overpriced, unnecessary, or just a smokescreen.
® Often, distributors end up buying the product themselves to meet sales quotas.
® In many cases, little to no actual sales to outside customers ever occur.

4. The Collapse

® Eventually, most people lose money because there aren't enough new recruits.
® Only those at the top of the chain (early entrants) make significant profits.
® The majority burn out, stuck with unsold inventory and financial losses.

Common MLM-to-Scam Red Flags

- Income from recruitment > income from product sales.
- Pressure to "go all in" and purchase high-priced starter packs.
- Compensation plans that are confusing or overly complicated.
- Fake lifestyle marketing: luxury cars, travel, vague claims about income.
- No clear evidence of real retail customers outside the distributor network.
- Cult-like language: "If you're not succeeding, it's because you didn't believe enough."

Real-World Examples

Herbalife was investigated by the FTC and paid $200 million in a settlement over misleading business claims.

LuLaRoe, a women's clothing MLM, left many consultants in debt with unsold inventory they were pressured to buy.

Some crypto-based MLMs disguise themselves as "investment platforms" but operate just like digital pyramid schemes.

How to Spot an MLM That's Functionally a Scam

- You're promised huge income "if you just recruit two people."
- Most people in the company don't make any profit, and the company's own income disclosure proves it.
- You're required to buy products monthly just to stay "active."
- Refunds are difficult or discouraged.
- Online reviews and former distributors describe it as "manipulative" or "a cult."

How to Protect Yourself

Research the company on FTC.gov or Better Business Bureau.

Read the income disclosure statement (if they have one). It often reveals how little most people earn.

Avoid businesses where your success is tied more to recruiting than selling.

Don't be pressured into buying more than you need or want.

Trust your gut. If it feels manipulative, it probably is.

Education & Scholarship Scams

- **Fake Degree Mills**

Selling worthless diplomas.

- **Scholarship Scams**

Charging for “guaranteed” grants.

- **Tutoring Scams**

Payment taken with no service rendered.

Fake Degree Mills: Buying a Diploma That's Not Worth the Paper It's Printed On

What Are Degree Mills?

Degree mills are fraudulent organizations that offer degrees, diplomas, or certificates with little to no academic work required. They may present themselves as legitimate universities, but they often lack accreditation, academic standards, and credibility. These scams exploit people's desire for quick credentials - whether for employment, immigration, or prestige.

How It Works

1. The Illusion of Legitimacy

® The degree mill sets up a professional-looking website, sometimes even using names similar to real universities.

® They claim to offer "life experience degrees," “fast-track diplomas,” or “international certifications.”

2. The Sales Pitch

® You’re told that you can earn a degree in days or weeks without attending classes or completing coursework.

® Some sites allow you to choose your GPA, graduation year, and even custom transcripts.

3. The Payment Trap

® A fee is required: usually anywhere from $150 to several thousand dollars.

® Some charge extra for transcripts, honors distinctions, verification services, or alumni privileges.

4. The Aftermath

® You receive a fake diploma, often mailed in a fancy folder with official-looking seals and signatures.

® The degree is useless for job applications, immigration, or academic advancement, and using it can even be illegal in some countries.

Common Variants

- Accreditation scams: Fake accrediting bodies are created to "certify" degree mills and make them seem legitimate.
- Religious or international institutions: Some claim to be global or faith-based universities operating under special legal exemptions.
- Doctorate mills: “Instant” PhDs, MBAs, or MDs for sale to boost your status.
- Honorary degree sales: Offering fake honorary degrees for a “donation.”

Red Flags to Watch For

- No coursework required, or you're "evaluated" based only on life experience.
- Institutions not recognized by your country's official education department or council.
- Degrees can be obtained in a few days or via online application only.
- Poor grammar and spelling on the website.
- Website lacks contact details or uses a Gmail/Hotmail address.

Real-World Examples

Axact, a Pakistan-based company, sold tens of thousands of fake diplomas under hundreds of fake university names.

In the U.S., people have been fired or prosecuted for listing fake degrees on résumés, especially in government or academic jobs.

Some job seekers unknowingly paid for fake degrees and were later denied employment or blacklisted.

How to Protect Yourself

Always check if the university is accredited by a legitimate education authority.

....

Use government-maintained databases to verify institutions (like U.S. Department of Education).

....

Beware of any academic institution that guarantees degrees or doesn't require coursework.

....

If applying for a job, remember that using a fake degree can lead to termination or legal charges.

....

Ask for reviews or experiences from real students or alumni. Degree mills usually can't provide this.

Scholarship Scams: Promises of Free Money That Cost You Instead

What Are Scholarship Scams?

Scholarship scams prey on students and parents looking for help with the rising cost of education. These scams promise guaranteed grants, financial aid, or scholarships - but end up charging fees, stealing personal data, or enrolling victims in worthless services. Many families fall victim out of urgency, not realizing that legitimate scholarships never ask you to pay upfront.

How It Works

1. The "You've Won!" Email or Call

® You receive a message saying you've been selected for a scholarship or grant.

® The offer sounds exclusive, urgent, and often comes from a name that sounds official (like the "National Scholarship Foundation").

2. The Catch: A Fee

® You're asked to pay a processing, application, or disbursement fee - often between $20 and $200.

® Some may also upsell "access to a scholarship database" or "guaranteed aid matching" services.

3. No Scholarship Ever Arrives

® After payment, communication stops, or you're strung along with endless requests for more info or additional fees.

® If you try to get your money back, the company disappears or refuses refunds.

4. Identity Theft Variant

® Some scammers ask for Social Security numbers, bank details, or student IDs, and later use them for identity fraud or phishing.

Common Variants

- Guaranteed awards: No scholarship is ever truly guaranteed.
- Pay-to-apply schemes: Charging a fee to "apply" for financial aid.
- Fake contests: You're told you won a scholarship you never applied for.
- Phishing forms: Designed to collect sensitive information under the guise of a "financial aid application."
- Seminar scams: You're invited to an "aid seminar" that turns into a high-pressure sales pitch for loan services.

Red Flags to Watch For

- “Guaranteed” scholarships or awards.
- Requests for payment, even small amounts, up front.
- You’re told you won an award you didn’t apply for.
- Requests for sensitive information like SSN, bank details, or login credentials.
- No real contact info, mailing address, or human support team.
- Overuse of official-sounding language or seals to appear government-backed.

Real-World Examples

The Federal Trade Commission (FTC) has prosecuted companies that collected millions in fees for fake or never-awarded scholarships.

Students have been tricked into paying $50 or more to access "exclusive databases" that contain only publicly available scholarships.

Some parents were told their child had won a $5,000 grant - then asked to pay a $200 "release fee."

How to Protect Yourself

Never pay to apply for a scholarship or access aid information.

Use trusted sources, like official government or university financial aid offices

Verify the legitimacy of any organization by checking reviews or searching "[organization name] scam."

Be skeptical of unsolicited offers: if it sounds too good to be true, it probably is.

Report scams to the FTC or your local education authority.

Tutoring Scams: Paying for Help That Never Comes

What Are Tutoring Scams?

Tutoring scams exploit students and parents who are seeking academic support. These frauds promise personalized tutoring services: sometimes for standardized tests, specific subjects, or homework help - but then deliver nothing, provide low-quality service, or simply vanish with your money. As demand for online tutoring grows, so do the scams.

How It Works

1. The Pitch

® You see an ad or get a call offering expert tutoring at "affordable rates."
® The website looks polished, maybe even with fake testimonials and fake tutor bios.
® Sometimes, scammers claim to be from reputable platforms like "Khan Academy partners" or "certified SAT experts."

2. Upfront Payment Required

® You're asked to prepay for a bundle of sessions, commonly 5, 10, or even 50 hours.
® The rates seem too good to be true - sometimes 50% off "for a limited time."

3. The Disappearing Act

® After payment, the tutor either:
§ Never shows up,
§ Constantly reschedules, or
§ Delivers such poor instruction it's useless.
® In some cases, you're ghosted completely: no refunds, no contact, no support.

4. Advanced Phishing Variant

® Some sites posing as tutoring services collect personal data and later use it for identity theft or spam attacks.

Common Variants

- Fake tutor profiles: Using stock images and made-up credentials.
- Lead generation scams: The site takes your info and sells it, without offering actual tutoring.
- Homework "help" sites: Offer to do assignments for a fee, then deliver plagiarized or incorrect work (or nothing at all).
- Scam apps: Mobile apps that charge subscription fees with no working service or way to cancel.

Red Flags to Watch For

- Prepayment required before even talking to a tutor.
- No video consultations or free trial session.
- No real contact info, only an email form or chat bot.
- Tutors refuse to give credentials or references.
- Overpromising: “Guaranteed A+ results!” or “Harvard-level tutors for $10/hr.”
- Pressure tactics like “limited slots” or “book today or lose your deal.”

Real-World Examples

Scammers posing as test prep centers during SAT season, charging hundreds for fake "college entrance coaching."

Facebook and Instagram ads leading to websites that collect prepayments for "live tutors" who never show.

Parents being tricked into monthly subscriptions they didn't knowingly sign up for - and can't cancel.

How to Protect Yourself

Ask for a free consultation or trial session before paying anything.

Research the platform: search “[name] + scam” or check Trustpilot/Reddit.

Use established platforms like Wyzant, Chegg, or your school’s official tutoring resources.

Avoid pre-paying for large packages unless the company has a clear, documented refund policy.

If using an individual tutor, ask for credentials, references, and a receipt.

Government-Related & Legal Scams

- **IRS/Tax Collection Scams**

Threatening legal action over "unpaid taxes."

- **Jury Duty Scams**

Claiming you missed jury duty and owe a fine.

- **Social Security Scams**

Claiming your SSN has been suspended.

- **Student Loan Forgiveness Scams**

Charging fees for free services.

IRS/Tax Collection Scams: Fear Tactics That Steal Your Money

What Are IRS/Tax Collection Scams?

These scams involve fraudsters posing as tax authorities: like the IRS (in the U.S.), HMRC (in the UK), or other national revenue agencies who threaten victims with arrest, lawsuits, or asset seizure over allegedly unpaid taxes. They rely heavily on fear and urgency, catching victims off guard, especially around tax season.

How It Works

1. The Scary Call or Message

® You receive a phone call, text, email, or even letter claiming you owe taxes.

® The tone is aggressive: you're threatened with arrest, lawsuit, asset freeze, or even deportation if you don't act immediately.

2. The Urgent Demand

® You're told to pay immediately using unconventional methods: prepaid debit cards, wire transfers, cryptocurrency, or gift cards.

® You're ordered not to hang up, talk to anyone, or verify anything with the actual IRS.

3. Emotional Pressure

® The scammer may give you a fake badge number, caller ID spoofing a real agency number, or even transfer you to a fake "supervisor."

® Victims are often kept on the phone for hours to prevent them from seeking help or thinking clearly.

Common Variants

- Robocalls: Automated voice messages that say your "tax case has been escalated."
- Email scams: Phishing emails with fake tax bills or refund notifications.
- Text message threats: "Final Notice" texts demanding payment or threatening asset seizure.
- Fake refund bait: You're told you're owed a tax refund, but must confirm your bank details first (classic phishing).

Red Flags to Watch For

- Call or message threatens arrest, lawsuits, or deportation over unpaid taxes.
- You're asked to pay via gift cards, crypto, or wire transfers.
- The caller demands immediate action and says you can't hang up or consult a lawyer.
- They won't let you call the agency back via its official public number.
- Emails or texts contain urgent language, misspellings, or suspicious links.

Real-World Examples

In the U.S., the IRS has repeatedly warned that it will never call you to demand immediate payment, yet thousands fall for these scams annually.

Victims have lost thousands of dollars in gift cards or wire transfers under the belief they were settling a tax debt.

Immigrants and the elderly are common targets, often tricked into thinking they'll be deported or jailed.

How to Protect Yourself

Know this: Legitimate tax agencies never demand immediate payment by phone or email, and they never accept gift cards or crypto.

Hang up and call the official agency number directly

Don't click on links in suspicious emails or texts claiming to be from the government.

Report scam attempts to the relevant government agency (e.g., TIGTA in the U.S.).

Educate family and elderly relatives, who are common targets.

Jury Duty Scams: "You Missed Jury Duty. Now Pay the Fine"

What Are Jury Duty Scams?

Jury duty scams are designed to exploit people's fear of legal trouble. Scammers pretend to be court officials, law enforcement, or government representatives and claim you missed a mandatory jury summons. You're then threatened with arrest, fines, or legal action unless you pay up immediately. These scams can feel very real, especially when the caller uses your full name, address, or spoofed government numbers.

How It Works

1. The Initial Call

® A scammer posing as a sheriff, court officer, or U.S. marshal calls you.

® They say you failed to appear for jury duty and now face serious consequences, such as arrest or suspension of your driver's license.

2. The Threat & Fake Solution

® You're told there's an active warrant out for your arrest.

® However, they say the warrant can be canceled if you pay a fine immediately, usually via gift cards, wire transfers, or prepaid debit cards.

3. High-Pressure Tactics

® They insist you must act now to avoid jail.

® You're told not to hang up, speak to anyone else, or verify with the courthouse.

Common Variants

- Fake citations sent via email or text to legitimize the claim.
- Scammers may ask for personal info under the guise of "verifying your identity" (used for identity theft).
- Some versions involve in-person visits by scammers impersonating law enforcement officers.
- Others may ask for payment for "court fees" related to jury duty "paperwork."

Red Flags to Watch For

- Unexpected calls claiming you missed jury duty.
- Threats of immediate arrest unless you pay over the phone.
- Requests for gift card codes, Zelle, Venmo, or wire transfers.
- Caller refuses to let you call the court directly.
- Overuse of urgent, official-sounding language and legal terms.

Real-World Examples

Victims have been tricked into paying hundreds or thousands in gift cards for "bail."

In several states, scammers used court-seal letterheads and forged arrest warrants to convince targets.

Some fraudsters have gone so far as to spoof local police department phone numbers to look legitimate.

How to Protect Yourself

Know this: Courts never call you to demand payment for missed jury duty, especially not via gift cards or over the phone.

Hang up and call your local courthouse directly using a verified number.

Don't give personal or financial info to unsolicited callers.

Report scams to your local police or government fraud reporting agency.

Warn friends and elderly relatives. This scam heavily targets seniors.

Social Security Scams: "Your SSN Has Been Suspended!"

What Are Social Security Scams?

Social Security scams target individuals by impersonating officials from agencies like the Social Security Administration (SSA). Scammers claim there is a problem with your Social Security Number (SSN), such as it being suspended, compromised, or linked to criminal activity, and they use this fabricated crisis to steal your money or identity.

How It Works

1. **The Alarm Call**

® You receive a call, voicemail, or robocall saying your SSN has been:
§ "Suspended due to suspicious activity,"
§ "Used in criminal operations," or
§ "Involved in a money laundering investigation."

2. **Scare Tactics & Urgency**

® You're told you must verify your identity to resolve the issue - or risk arrest, asset seizure, or loss of benefits.
® Sometimes you're pressured into staying on the phone while following instructions.

3. **The Scam Unfolds**

® You're asked for your full SSN, banking info, or other personal details.
® Some are instructed to withdraw money and transfer it via gift cards, wire transfers, or cryptocurrency to "secure it" while the issue is being resolved.
® The scammer might even transfer you to a "supervisor" to make it feel more real.

Common Variants

- Caller ID spoofing makes it look like the call is from "SSA," "Government Services," or "Federal Office."
- Robocalls with urgent messages like: "Press 1 to speak with an agent."
- Fake emails or texts with SSA logos and links to phishing sites.
- Claims that your SSN was used to rent a car that was found with drugs or weapons - now you're implicated unless you "cooperate."

Red Flags to Watch For

- Threats of SSN suspension, arrest, or asset seizure.
- Requests for your full Social Security Number or bank details over the phone.
- Pressure to act immediately, especially using untraceable payment methods.
- Claims that your SSN is linked to criminal activity.
- Emails with official-looking logos but odd grammar, spelling mistakes, or sketchy links.

Real-World Examples

In 2020 alone, the U.S. reported over 700,000 complaints of Social Security scams, with losses totaling tens of millions.

Seniors are especially targeted, with scammers claiming their benefits will be suspended unless they comply.

Some victims have lost entire savings by "protecting" money through transfers to scammers.

How to Protect Yourself

Know this: The SSA never calls to threaten arrest or demand immediate payment.

If you get a suspicious call, hang up and call the SSA directly

---

Never give out your full SSN or banking info to unsolicited callers.

If unsure, ask for the caller's name, agency, and callback number. Then independently verify it.

Report scams.

Student Loan Forgiveness Scams: False Promises, Real Losses

What Are Student Loan Forgiveness Scams?

These scams target individuals with student debt by offering fake "forgiveness" programs, debt relief, or faster access to government aid - for a fee. Scammers often pose as official representatives of the Department of Education or other government entities, using urgent messages to lure borrowers into paying for services that are free or non-existent.

How It Works

1. The Bait: Loan Forgiveness or Reduced Payments

® You receive a call, email, text, or social media ad promising quick access to loan forgiveness under new government programs.
® You're told you're eligible for debt elimination, consolidation, or reduced payments, but you must act fast to lock in the deal.

2. The Hook: Upfront Fees

® Scammers claim they can:

- Cancel your loan for a fee,
- Consolidate your debt "faster" than the government,
- Enroll you in a "special program" for $500–$1,500.

3. The Trap: Identity Theft or Abandonment

® They ask for your FSA ID, SSN, income info, or banking details.
® After payment, they either:

- Disappear,
- Provide no real service, or
- Enroll you in a legitimate free program, but now they control your account.

Common Variants

- "Limited-time offer" forgiveness programs claiming to expire soon.
- Messages saying "Your student loan payments will resume unless you act now."
- Fake websites mimicking the real website with slight spelling differences.
- Promises of "debt erasure" under non-existent programs like the "Biden Student Relief Fund."

Red Flags to Watch For

- Requests for upfront payment to access loan forgiveness or consolidation.
- Promises that sound too good to be true - like full cancellation without conditions.
- Claims of "special access" to federal programs.
- Urgency: "Act now before the program ends!" or "You must enroll today!"
- Suspicious websites or email domains that don't end in .gov.

Real-World Examples

Many scammers surfaced after the announcement of student loan pauses or relief plans, tricking borrowers into urgent decisions.

Victims have lost hundreds to thousands of dollars in upfront fees.

Some gave away their FSA ID credentials, allowing scammers to reroute communications and control their loan accounts.

How to Protect Yourself

Never pay to apply for student loan forgiveness or consolidation. Federal programs are free.

Don't share your FSA ID, SSN, or banking info with unsolicited callers or websites.

Verify the legitimacy of any offer by contacting your loan servicer directly.

Report scams to the FTC or your state attorney general's office.

Health & Wellness Scams

- **Miracle Cures & Supplements**

Products that don't work, sold with false medical claims.

- **Fake Insurance Scams**

Offering bogus policies.

- **Stem Cell / Anti-Aging Frauds**

Targeting vulnerable patients.

Miracle Cures & Supplements: Hope in a Bottle, Lies on the Label

What Are Miracle Cure Scams?

These scams involve the sale of products that claim to cure or prevent serious illnesses (like cancer, diabetes, Alzheimer's, or COVID-19) without scientific proof or FDA approval. They're often marketed as "natural," "ancient," or "secret" remedies, promising fast results with no side effects. Victims not only lose money, but they may delay real treatment and put their health at risk.

How It Works

1. False Promise of a Cure

® Scammers market pills, powders, creams, teas, or devices as miracle solutions for incurable or chronic diseases.

® The product is usually sold online, via spam emails, late-night infomercials, or social media influencers.

2. Emotional Appeal

® Claims are often wrapped in emotive language, fake testimonials, and phrases like:

- "Big Pharma doesn't want you to know this."
- "Clinically proven by ancient science."
- "Doctors hate this natural cure."

3. High Cost for False Hope

® Victims pay hundreds to thousands of dollars for these "life-changing" cures - often shipped from abroad or never delivered at all.

® Some schemes set up auto-renewing charges without consent.

Common Variants

- CBD scams promising to treat everything from arthritis to cancer.
- “Alkaline water” or “miracle minerals” claimed to neutralize disease.
- Fake weight loss supplements with photoshopped before-and-after images.
- Products marketed as “not FDA approved but used for decades.”

Red Flags to Watch For

- Phrases like "cure-all," "instant results," "100% safe," or "doctors won't tell you this."
- Lack of credible scientific studies or links to peer-reviewed journals.
- No contact information, refund policy, or company history.
- Testimonials that sound scripted or exaggerated.
- The product is only available through a single website with countdown timers or "limited stock" warnings.

Real-World Examples

The FDA and FTC regularly send warnings to companies selling “cures” for cancer, COVID-19, and more without evidence.

In one case, scammers sold bleach-based products as a “miracle mineral solution.”

Social media has seen waves of influencers promoting false cures, some of which caused severe harm.

How to Protect Yourself

Always consult a licensed medical professional before trying new treatments or supplements.

Research any product on official sites.

Be skeptical of emotional marketing or fear-based claims.

Check if the supplement is listed in clinical trials or has been flagged by watchdog organizations.

Report scammy products to the FDA's MedWatch or the Better Business Bureau (BBB).

Fake Insurance Scams: Coverage That Doesn't Exist

What Are Fake Insurance Scams?

These scams involve criminals or shady companies selling nonexistent or useless health insurance policies - usually targeting individuals who are uninsured, self-employed, elderly, or desperate for affordable coverage. Victims believe they're buying real protection, only to discover (often too late) that the policy is worthless or fake.

How It Works

1. The Offer of "Affordable" Coverage

® Scammers advertise low-cost or comprehensive health insurance with immediate approval, no medical exams, or guaranteed acceptance.
® These offers are often promoted through telemarketing calls, online ads, or fake enrollment websites - especially around open enrollment seasons.

2. The Sign-Up Trap

® You're rushed into enrolling, often told "spaces are limited" or that "the deal ends today."
® Victims are asked to pay an enrollment fee or monthly premium via wire transfer, prepaid card, or ACH debit.
® You may receive fake documents, cards, or logins that appear legitimate.

3. The Moment of Truth

® When you try to use the insurance, you find out:

- The provider doesn't exist.
- The plan doesn't cover anything meaningful.
- The policy was a discount plan, not actual insurance.
- There's no customer service, or the number has been disconnected.

Common Variants

- Policies misrepresented as "Obamacare-compliant" or "government-backed."
- "Health share ministries" presented as full insurance but with no guarantees of payment.
- Scammers posing as ACA navigators or Medicare agents who are actually unlicensed.

Red Flags to Watch For

- Pressure to act immediately or risk missing out.

- Claims like:

1. "Covers everything from prescriptions to surgery, no questions asked."
2. "You don't need to go through the marketplace."

- §Requests for upfront payment via unusual methods (gift card, wire, crypto).

- §No clear explanation of deductibles, copays, or provider networks.

- §Websites that look generic or mimic real government sites (e.g., ending in ".org" instead of ".gov").

Real-World Examples

The FTC has busted multiple operations that scammed thousands into paying for junk insurance plans that were nothing more than discount card programs.

Some schemes used names that sounded official, like "National Health Enrollment Center" or "Federal Health Plans."

How to Protect Yourself

Verify insurance plans and agents through your state's insurance department.

Be cautious of any plan that seems far cheaper than competitors.

Use official channels for real options.

Ask for a Summary of Benefits and Coverage (SBC) and check the company's NAIC number.

Never give out personal or payment info unless you are certain the source is legitimate.

Stem Cell / Anti-Aging Frauds Science-Washed Scams for the Desperate

What Are Stem Cell and Anti-Aging Scams?

These scams exploit hope and fear by offering unproven or illegal medical treatments, especially targeting the elderly, chronically ill, or beauty-conscious. They often promise miraculous results (from regenerating organs to reversing aging) with stem cell therapy, regenerative injections, or age-defying elixirs. In reality, these treatments are often completely ineffective, dangerously experimental, or outright fake.

How It Works

1. The Pseudoscience Pitch

® Scammers advertise stem cell or anti-aging products as cutting-edge science, often claiming:
§ "Clinically proven to regenerate tissue."
§ "Reverses aging at the cellular level."
§ "Used by celebrities and athletes."

2. The Emotional Hook

® Ads target people dealing with:
- Chronic pain
- Neurological conditions
- Memory loss
- Wrinkles or skin aging

® Victims are shown dramatic before-and-after images and testimonials - usually fake or misleading.

3. The Price of False Hope

® Treatments may be offered at thousands of dollars per session, with no insurance coverage.
® Some operations occur in unlicensed "clinics" in the U.S. or overseas.
® Patients often receive placebos, contaminated products, or nothing at all.

Common Variants

- Stem cell injections for arthritis, spine problems, or MS.
- Anti-aging creams or serums claiming DNA regeneration.
- "Regenerative therapy packages" combining supplements, light therapy, and injections.
- Clinics promoting “exosome” treatments or “cord blood therapies” without FDA clearance.

Red Flags to Watch For

- Terms like "miracle cure," "guaranteed results," or "clinically proven," with no supporting data.
- No mention of FDA approval or legitimate clinical trials.
- The treatment is only available in certain states or countries, claiming U.S. laws "get in the way of healing."
- Pressure to pay upfront, or pay out of pocket for multiple sessions.
- Refusal to provide detailed risks or side effects.

Real-World Examples

The FDA has cracked down on several clinics selling unproven stem cell treatments that left patients blinded or seriously injured.

Celebrities endorsing stem cell therapy have helped fuel false legitimacy, even when science does not support their claims.

Some overseas "medical tourism" clinics charge tens of thousands for unregulated procedures with no oversight.

How to Protect Yourself

Check the FDA's warning list for unapproved stem cell clinics and products.

Always ask: Is there peer-reviewed research or a clinical trial supporting this treatment?

Avoid any medical treatment that requires you to travel abroad without oversight or consultation.

Don't assume a product is safe just because it's marketed as "natural" or "regenerative."

Consult a licensed medical professional or specialist before pursuing any advanced treatment.

Tech & Digital Scams

- **NFT Scams**

Selling stolen artwork or non-existent digital assets.

- **AI Job/Content Scams**

Claiming to pay for AI-generated content, then ghosting.

- **Deepfake Blackmail**

Faking compromising videos/photos.

- **Fake App Scams**

Apps that steal data or plant malware.

- **QR Code Scams**

Malicious codes redirecting to phishing sites.

NFT Scams – When "Owning Digital Art" Becomes a Digital Trap

What Are NFT Scams?

NFTs (Non-Fungible Tokens) exploded in popularity as a way to buy and sell digital ownership of art, music, or collectibles. But where there's hype, there are scams. NFT scams involve selling stolen, fake, or non-existent NFTs, or manipulating users into giving up control of their crypto wallets.

The result? People pay for assets that are worthless, vanish, or were never legitimate in the first place.

How It Works

1. Stolen or Fake Artwork

® Scammers copy an artist's work and mint it as their own NFT.
® Buyers unknowingly purchase the stolen asset, which holds no legitimate value.

2. Rug Pull Projects

® Fraudsters launch an NFT collection with big promises (e.g., future utility, games, metaverse).
® After the project sells out, the team disappears, deleting social media and taking the money.

3. Phishing via "Airdrops" or Links

® You receive a free NFT or a message offering a rare item.
® Clicking the link or connecting your wallet triggers malware or authorizes transactions that drain your funds.

4. Pump-and-Dump Hype

® Influencers or insiders artificially boost the price of an NFT collection.
® Once it spikes, they sell off their holdings, and the floor price crashes, leaving latecomers with losses.

Common Variants

- Fake marketplaces mimicking OpenSea or Magic Eden.
- Impersonation of famous artists or influencers.
- “Giveaway” scams on Twitter, Discord, or Telegram asking for wallet access.
- NFT projects offering unrealistic returns or passive income.

Red Flags to Watch For

- The project team is anonymous or hard to verify.
- You're asked to connect your wallet just to view or claim something.
- Promises of huge returns, staking rewards, or guaranteed profits.
- Pressure to act fast before "minting ends" or "supply runs out."
- Unusual URLs or slight misspellings in marketplace domains.

Real-World Examples

Artists like Loish and Qinni had their works minted and sold without consent.

The "Evolved Apes" NFT project raised over $2 million, then disappeared without delivering anything.

Numerous OpenSea users lost NFTs due to phishing links disguised as site updates or airdrops.

How to Protect Yourself

Only buy NFTs from verified platforms (e.g., OpenSea, Rarible, Foundation).

Double-check artist profiles and confirm the authenticity of listings.

Never click on unknown links sent via DMs or emails.

Use a separate wallet for NFT transactions with limited funds.

Treat NFTs like speculative assets, not guaranteed investments.

AI Job/Content Scams – Fake Gigs in the Age of Automation

What Are AI Job/Content Scams?

As AI tools like ChatGPT, Midjourney, and DALL·E gain traction, so do scammers exploiting them. These scams offer fake job opportunities to people looking to earn money creating AI-generated content: text, art, or videos. Victims are lured in with promises of easy pay, only to be ghosted, tricked into paying fees, or used as free labor.

How It Works

1. Fake AI Job Listings

® Scammers post on freelance platforms, job boards, or Discord communities offering gigs like:

- “Write 100 AI articles and earn $500.”
- “Generate 50 images with Midjourney for our startup.”

® Victims complete the work, submit it, and are never paid.

2. Training or Access Fees

® Some scammers claim you must pay for training, buy a license, or upgrade to a premium AI tool to qualify.

® Once you pay, communication stops, or you’re looped into more fake tasks.

3. Harvesting Free Content

® Victims are tricked into producing high volumes of content for a fake “project test.”

® Scammers steal the content and resell or use it elsewhere.

4. Affiliate and Pyramid Traps

® Some scammers say you can earn money by recruiting others to use a particular AI tool - often a pyramid model in disguise.

Common Variants

- Fake publishing companies offering "ghostwriting contracts."
- "Earn $200/day using ChatGPT!" ads that link to spammy programs.
- Websites promising passive income from AI-generated YouTube channels.
- Telegram/Reddit groups that send bulk job offers with shady links.

Red Flags to Watch For

- Vague project details but high pay promises.
- You're asked to "prove yourself" by completing large unpaid sample tasks.
- Job offers through unsolicited DMs or social media posts.
- Upfront charges for "training," "AI licenses," or "membership."
- No company info, no contract, no payment timeline.

Real-World Examples

Dozens of Reddit users report falling for "ChatGPT blog writing" jobs that never paid and ghosted after submission.

Some scammy platforms rebrand open-source AI tools, then charge people for access under the pretense of "work opportunities."

AI art communities have flagged "clients" who mass-request images, then disappear after download.

How to Protect Yourself

Only accept jobs from verified clients on legitimate freelance platforms.

Never pay to work. Real employers pay you, not the other way around.

Reverse search any company name or offer to check for scam reports.

Keep sample submissions short and watermarked when possible.

Avoid jobs that require massive upfront effort without any contract or commitment.

Deepfake Blackmail – When Fake Videos Become Real Threats

What Is Deepfake Blackmail?

Deepfake blackmail involves scammers using AI-generated images or videos, often explicit or compromising, to threaten, extort, or manipulate victims. With AI tools now capable of generating incredibly realistic faces and voices, it's easier than ever for bad actors to fake a video or photo and demand money to prevent its release.

This scam combines psychological pressure, digital impersonation, and privacy invasion to create fear and compliance.

How It Works

1. Image Harvesting

® Scammers find your photos from social media, school or work websites, or video content.

® These images are fed into AI tools to create deepfake videos or nude photos of you.

2. Blackmail Threat

® You receive a message (often by email or social media) claiming:

- "We created this video of you."
- "We will send this to your friends/family if you don't pay."

® Sometimes they attach screenshots or even snippets to make the threat feel real.

3. Payment Demand

® The scammer demands money in crypto or gift cards to "delete the video" or "stay silent."

® In some cases, payment only leads to further extortion.

4. Emotional Manipulation

® These scams often target teens, professionals, or influencers, knowing reputational damage can be severe.

® The fear of exposure causes victims to act before verifying the truth.

Common Variants

- Sextortion emails with fake claims like "I hacked your webcam" or "You visited an adult site."
- Social media impersonation: scammers create fake accounts with altered images.
- Targeted harassment of public figures or content creators with edited "leaks."

Red Flags to Watch For

- You receive an unsolicited message claiming they have a video or photo of you.
- The message includes a threat of exposure and a demand for payment.
- They push for fast payment in crypto or untraceable methods.
- Email or social media accounts appear suspicious, new, or mismatched.

Real-World Examples

In 2023, multiple students and influencers reported deepfake pornographic content of themselves being circulated without consent.

FBI issued warnings about deepfake extortion after reports of false videos used to bully minors and extort adults.

Some scammers combined phishing attacks with deepfakes - first stealing credentials, then faking content.

How to Protect Yourself

Don't panic. Most blackmailers are bluffing with fake content.

Do not pay. Payment often makes you a repeat target.

Report and block the account immediately.

Save the evidence: screenshots, email headers, usernames, etc.

Contact authorities (cybercrime divisions or hotlines) or support organizations.

Use strong privacy settings on social media and avoid sharing personal visuals publicly.

Deepfake technology can be terrifying in the wro hands, but knowledge and calm action are your stronge shields.

Fake App Scams – Malicious Apps in Disguise

What Are Fake App Scams?

Fake app scams involve malicious or deceptive mobile applications that trick users into downloading them under false pretenses. These apps might promise a useful function: like a flashlight, game, health tracker, or finance tool - but actually aim to steal your data, plant malware, or drain your bank account.

Some fake apps even appear on official app stores, making them seem trustworthy at first glance.

How It Works

1. The Bait

® The app appears in an ad, social media post, or even on Google Play/App Store.

® It might claim to do something attractive like:

- "Get rich using AI tools!"
- "Scan QR codes with military-grade security!"
- "Exclusive deals just for you!"

2. The Trap

® Once installed, the app:

- Requests excessive permissions (access to contacts, camera, SMS, etc.).
- Redirects you to phishing pages.
- Installs malware that logs keystrokes or accesses banking apps.

3. The Damage

® Your personal and financial information is stolen.

® You may be signed up for premium subscriptions you didn't authorize.

® In some cases, the phone is completely locked or hijacked for ransom (ransomware).

Common Variants

- Fake banking apps that mimic legitimate banks.
- Crypto wallet apps that steal login credentials.
- Loan apps that harvest personal data and demand repayments on non-existent loans.
- Child-targeted games with hidden in-app purchases or inappropriate ads.
- “Security” apps that are actually spyware.

Red Flags to Watch For

- Poor grammar or broken English in app description.
- Suspicious developer name or vague contact info.
- Excessive permissions (e.g., why does a calculator need access to your microphone?).
- Very few or overwhelmingly positive reviews (often fake).
- The app suddenly disappears from the store after installation.

Real-World Examples

In 2021, Google removed over 200+ apps from the Play Store that were harvesting user data or sending users to scam websites.

A wave of fake cryptocurrency wallet apps stole millions of dollars from victims by tricking them into entering real wallet credentials.

Some apps promised COVID-19 contact tracing or vaccination records but were loaded with malware.

How to Protect Yourself

Only download apps from official app stores (Google Play, Apple App Store).

Check the developer name, app size, and version history.

Read multiple real reviews: look for patterns of complaints or warnings.

Use a reliable mobile antivirus or security app to scan new installations.

Avoid clicking download links in random ads or messages.

Review and restrict app permissions in your phone settings.

Fake apps often look legitimate, but under the hood, th can be devastating. A few seconds of caution can sa your device, your identity, and your money.

QR Code Scams – The Hidden Danger in a Simple Square

What Are QR Code Scams?

QR code scams involve criminals placing malicious or misleading QR codes in public or digital spaces. When scanned, these codes may lead to phishing sites, install malware, or trick you into entering sensitive information. Because QR codes are unreadable by the human eye, people trust them blindly, making them an ideal tool for scammers.

How It Works

1. The Setup

® Scammers generate a fraudulent QR code that leads to:

- A fake login page for a bank or payment app.
- A malicious app download link.
- A spoofed cryptocurrency wallet address.
- A fake Wi-Fi login portal.

2. The Distribution

® QR codes are placed:

- On parking meters or gas pumps.
- On flyers or posters for events or promotions.
- In phishing emails or scam texts.
- In fake restaurant menus or delivery apps.

3. The Trap

® You scan the code expecting convenience.

® Instead, you might:

- Enter login or payment info on a phishing page.
- Have spyware or a trojan downloaded onto your device.
- Transfer crypto to a scammer's wallet.
- Give access to your camera, contacts, or GPS.

Common Variants

- Parking scams: Fake QR codes on meters redirect to phishing sites.
- Delivery scams: QR codes in fake missed delivery texts lead to fake tracking pages.
- Crypto scams: Codes link to a fake exchange or wallet, replacing your payment address.
- Business impersonation: Fake flyers for giveaways, sales, or restaurant menus.

Red Flags to Watch For

- A QR code in an unexpected location (e.g., a random sticker on a pole or ATM).
- Codes that don't show a clear, readable URL preview before opening.
- A website that asks for personal or payment info after scanning.
- A restaurant or shop QR code that looks like a sticker rather than printed.
- QR codes in emails or texts from unknown senders.

Real-World Examples

In several U.S. cities, scammers stuck fake QR code stickers on parking meters, tricking users into paying “fines” to the wrong account.

Restaurants during COVID posted QR menus, some of which were hijacked by scammers to install malware or redirect payments.

In one crypto phishing campaign, scammers used QR codes to replace legitimate wallet addresses and reroute user funds.

How to Protect Yourself

Preview links before opening them. Most smartphones show the URL first.

Only scan QR codes from trusted and verified sources.

Use a QR code scanner app with built-in security features.

Don't scan random public stickers or codes unless you trust their origin.

Watch for tampering. Scammers often place fake QR stickers over real ones.

Avoid entering sensitive info on websites opened via QR codes unless you're 100% sure they're legit.

QR Code Scams

QR codes offer convenience, but scammers exploit th invisibility. Stay alert, check the source, and never sc blindly.

Disaster & Charity Scams

- **Fake Charity Scams**

Especially after natural disasters or crises.

- **Crowdfunding Fraud**

Fake GoFundMe pages.

Fake Charity Scams – Exploiting Goodwill During Crisis

What Are Fake Charity Scams?

Fake charity scams take advantage of your generosity and empathy, especially after natural disasters, pandemics, or global tragedies. These scammers create phony organizations, websites, or donation pages that look legitimate but funnel the money into their own pockets instead of helping anyone in need.

How It Works

1. Triggering a Crisis

® A disaster strikes: a hurricane, earthquake, war, or humanitarian crisis.

® Scammers rush to exploit the moment, creating fake charities or posing as existing ones.

2. Spreading the Appeal

® You see emotional messages and images on:

- Social media (Twitter, Facebook, Instagram).
- Emails and text messages.
- Websites and crowdfunding platforms.
- Even phone calls from fake "volunteers."

3. Collecting the Funds

® Victims are urged to donate quickly, often via:

- Bank transfers.
- Untraceable methods like crypto or gift cards.
- Fake donation forms that also steal your identity.

Common Variants

- Impersonating real charities: Slight name changes or spoofed websites.
- Fake religious or military aid groups: “Support our troops” or “Help displaced families.”
- Scams around recent tragedies: Earthquakes, floods, school shootings, etc.
- Emotional images or testimonials with no verifiable information.
- Pressure tactics: “We need your help now! Lives are at stake!”

Red Flags to Watch For

- Vague organization names like "Disaster Relief International" with no history.
- Pressure to give immediately or via untraceable methods.
- Websites lacking details, transparency, or donation receipts.
- No mention of tax-deductible status or registration info.
- Poor grammar or strange URLs (e.g., .xyz or .info domains).

Real-World Examples

After the 2010 Haiti earthquake and again after Hurricane Katrina, hundreds of fake charities popped up, some collecting tens of thousands of dollars.

Following Russia's invasion of Ukraine, many phony fundraising pages on social media targeted people with emotional appeals and false promises.

During COVID-19, scammers ran fake charities promising PPE for hospitals or aid for families.

How to Protect Yourself

Verify before donating: Use charity watchdogs like Charity Navigator, Guidestar, or the IRS nonprofit list.

Avoid giving through links sent by text or social media unless verified.

Check for official websites, real contact info, and donation transparency.

Don't scan random public stickers or codes unless you trust their origin.

If approached by phone, hang up and call the organization directly.

Pay via secure, trackable methods, not crypto, gift cards, or wire transfers.

Fake Charity Scams

Scammers prey on compassion, turning crisis into profit. The best way to help? Give smart, give verified, and give without being rushed.

Crowdfunding Fraud – Fake GoFundMe Pages & Emotional Manipulation

What Is Crowdfunding Fraud?

Crowdfunding fraud occurs when scammers create fake fundraisers on platforms like GoFundMe, Kickstarter, or Indiegogo, using fabricated stories to solicit donations. These scams exploit empathy, trending causes, or even personal tragedies to collect money under false pretenses - and then vanish with the funds.

How It Works

1. The Setup

® A scammer invents:

- A fake medical emergency.
- A tragic accident or disaster story.
- A made-up business dream or invention.
- A fabricated humanitarian cause.

2. Building the Page

® The fraudster:

- Uses stolen or AI-generated photos.
- Writes a heartfelt, emotional story.
- Sets a modest donation goal to appear genuine.
- Shares it rapidly on social media, Reddit, or via email chains.
-

3. Taking the Money

® Once donations start rolling in:

- The scammer may disable comments to avoid scrutiny.
- They disappear once they've reached a certain amount.
- Sometimes they repeat the scam under different names or stories.

Common Variants

- Fake medical emergencies: Often claiming a child needs urgent surgery or treatment.
- Disaster exploitation: "We lost everything in the fire/flood" - complete fiction.
- Pet scams: "My dog needs surgery" stories with stolen animal photos.
- Startup fraud: Pretending to launch a business or invention that doesn't exist.
- Memorial fund hoaxes: Setting up a fake death/funeral donation page.

Red Flags to Watch For

- No verifiable personal details or updates on the page.
- Photos that look stock-like or unrelated (reverse image search helps).
- Strange campaign timelines, like being set up suspiciously fast after a disaster.
- Poor grammar, overly emotional language, and no transparency on how funds will be used.
- Comments or updates disabled without explanation.
- The organizer refuses to answer questions publicly or privately.

Real-World Examples

A woman in New Jersey raised over $400,000 in a viral GoFundMe scam involving a fake story about a homeless veteran. All parties involved were later charged with fraud.

During wildfires, scammers launched dozens of fake fundraisers, claiming to be displaced families or wildlife rescuers.

In 2020, multiple COVID-related campaigns emerged claiming to need PPE or cover medical bills. Many were completely fabricated.

How to Protect Yourself

Research before donating:

- Check if the story is reported in legitimate news sources.
- Look for updates and transparency in fund allocation.

Use platform reporting tools if something seems off.

Reverse-search any photos used to catch stolen images.

Favor verified campaigns, especially if promoted by trusted organizations.

If donating to someone you know personally, confirm their situation directly.

Scammers prey on compassion, turning crisis into profit. The best way to help? Give smart, give verified, and give without being rushed.

Final Words:

The Evolving Nature of Scams

Scams are not static, they evolve as technology advances, economies shift, and new vulnerabilities emerge. Just as we've adapted to new ways of living, scammers adapt to exploit those changes. From handwritten chain letters to AI-powered impersonations, the core principle remains the same: manipulation for profit.

What worked to protect you five years ago may not work today. That's why it's crucial to stay informed, stay skeptical, and never let your guard down entirely. Scammers rely on complacency, urgency, and misplaced trust. The best defense? Awareness and caution, practiced consistently.

Above all, don't let fear rule your life. Let knowledge empower you. By understanding how scams work and recognizing their patterns, you can outsmart even the most sophisticated schemes.

What to Do If You've Been Scammed

Realizing you've been scammed can feel overwhelming. But taking fast, deliberate action can minimize the damage and sometimes even help others avoid the same fate. Here's what to do:

1. Stop Further Contact

Cease communication with the scammer immediately. Don't send more money or respond to follow-up messages.

2. Document Everything

Save emails, texts, receipts, website URLs, usernames, and screenshots. This evidence may help investigators or support a refund claim.

3. Report the Scam

Depending on your country, report to relevant authorities:

- United States: FTC (ReportFraud.ftc.gov), IC3.gov (for cybercrime)
- UK: Action Fraud
- Canada: Canadian Anti-Fraud Centre
- Australia: Scamwatch
- International: Report to your bank, card provider, or payment platform.

4. Contact Your Bank or Payment Provider

Dispute the transaction or freeze your account if needed. Some banks may reverse charges if reported promptly.

5. Change Affected Passwords & Secure Your Info

Update login credentials for any compromised accounts. Consider enabling two-factor authentication (2FA).

6. Warn Others

Share your experience to help friends, family, or online communities avoid falling for the same trap.

How to Keep Learning and Stay Safe

Staying safe isn't about paranoia, it's about proactive learning. Here are steps you can take to build your scam immunity:

Stay Informed:

® Subscribe to scam alert newsletters (e.g., FTC Scam Alerts, local consumer protection agencies).

® Follow cybersecurity news to stay ahead of digital threats.

Practice Digital Hygiene:

® Use strong, unique passwords for each account.

® Enable 2FA on your most important accounts.

® Keep software and devices updated.

Question Urgency & Emotion:

® If a message or offer is urgent, emotional, or secretive, it's likely a red flag.

® Always take time to verify before acting.

Educate Others:

® Talk to family and friends - especially older adults and teens -about scams.

® Share reliable resources and stories without shame.

STAY SAFE

www.ingramcontent.com/pod-product-compliance
Lightning Source LLC
LaVergne TN
LVHW090311210926
848480LV00001B/207
9798231748150